THE LATIN MASS AND THE YOUTH

THE LATIN MASS AND THE YOUTH

Young Catholics Speak About the Mass of Ages

EDITED BY
REYERS P. BRUSCOE

Foreword by Peter Kwasniewski

Cruachan
Hill Press

First published in the USA
by Cruachan Hill Press 2024
Copyright Cruachan Hill Press © 2024

All rights reserved:
No part of this book may be reproduced or transmitted,
in any form or by any means, without permission

For information, address:
Cruachan Hill Press
12552 E. Michigan Ave
Grass Lake, MI 49240

paper 978-1-957206-31-8

Book design by Michael Schrauzer
Cover photo courtesy of Allison Girone
Cover design by Jessica Fellmeth

CONTENTS

Foreword ix
Editor's Introduction xvii

1 Utterly Fascinated 3
2 Beauty Rediscovered 6
3 A Nitty-Gritty Trad 8
4 Truth, Goodness, and Beauty 11
5 Like Falling in Love 13
6 The Incomparable Beauty of the
   Traditional Liturgy's Music 16
7 Seeking the Gifts of the Lord 19
8 "In the Presence of God!" 23
9 Everything Points to God 26
10 Serving at the Traditional Latin Mass 30
11 The Glorious Harmony and Sanctity
   of the Traditional Latin Mass 33
12 "He's Not a Tame Lion" 41
13 May the Latin Mass Live Forever 43
14 First and Lasting Impressions of
   the Traditional Latin Mass 46
15 The Serenity of the Traditional Latin Mass 49
16 "The Latin Mass Brings Peace to My Heart" 52
17 Amazement at the Sacrifice of Jesus 54
18 A Beautiful Harmony of Praise to the Lord 57
19 "My Soul Was Dying of Starvation Before" 59
20 Love and Sacrifice:
   A Betrothed Couple's Experience of the TLM 62
21 A Suspiciously Genuine Joy 65
22 Life on Fire 70

23	To Understand the Real Meaning of Sacrifice	73
24	The Cure This World Is in Dire Need Of	76
25	The Beautiful Poetry of Latin	79
26	The Mystery Before Which One Trembles	82
27	The Big Crossover	86
28	"Rapid Growth in My Spiritual Life"	89
29	A Server's Experience of the Traditional Mass	94
30	"Why Did They Ever Change It?"	98
31	Transformed by Tradition: A Jewish Convert's Journey	101
32	No Longer a Lost Sheep	105
33	The Traditional Mass is a "Reality Check"	110
34	God, Who Giveth Joy to My Youth	113
35	Wherever We Go, The Mass is Home	117
36	The Latin Mass Builds Community	120
37	Why Young Catholics Devote Themselves to the Traditional Latin Mass	123
38	Discovering the Ancient Mass Through an Accident	126
39	Late Have I Loved Thee	130
40	Truly Transformatory	133
41	A Mass That Was Never-Changing	137
42	The Latin Mass as the Church's Una Voce	141

FOREWORD

SERIOUS CATHOLIC YOUTHS CRAVE TRADITION —AND WE SHOULD LISTEN TO THEM

by Dr. Peter Kwasniewski

OVER THE CENTURIES, SEEKERS OF GOD HAVE often returned to the *Rule* of St. Benedict as a repository of timeless wisdom, capable of guiding any community to peace and holiness. One cannot help but be struck by the way Benedict emphasizes that the young monks' voices ought to be given a fair hearing. Benedict was not exactly egalitarian (he frequently counsels the beating of the refractory, for example), but he recognized, with St. John Cassian, that age does not automatically equal wisdom and that young people can have the perspective needed by the community at a given moment. Thus, he stipulates in chapter 63: "On no occasion whatsoever should age distinguish the brethren and decide their order [in the monastery]; for Samuel and Daniel, though young, judged the elders."[1] In chapter 3, the patriarch legislates:

> As often as any important business has to be done in the monastery, let the abbot call together the whole community and himself set forth the matter. And, having heard the advice of the brethren, let him take counsel with himself and then do what he shall judge to be most expedient. Now the reason why we have said that all should be called to council is that God often reveals what is better to the younger.[2]

The saint's advice seems all the more relevant in today's Church, when it is clearly the young who are rediscovering Catholic Tradition in all its fullness, and who, at the same time, are bearing the full brunt of the resistance of their elders, who have been "sticks in the mud" when it comes to welcoming this stirring of the Holy Spirit. In this curious way, today's older generations often seem like the Jews in the Gospels, who cannot receive the newness of Christ and his apostles.[3]

---

[1] In the bilingual McCann edition, p. 143.
[2] McCann ed., 25.
[3] See Acts 7:51.

It need hardly be said that St. Benedict's advice applies perfectly to monasteries, convents, and other religious houses, where, let us be frank about it, revival or even bare survival is bound up with a recovery of traditional liturgy, in both the Divine Office and the Mass, and in the chant.[4] It is no longer a secret that the most flourishing communities today are the ones that have unashamedly restored the way of life a foolish generation threw away in the name of *aggiornamento*. A Benedictine monk once told me that in the late 1960s, when his monastery switched over to a liturgy entirely in the vernacular, a member of the community actually put all of the copies of the *Antiphonale Monasticum* into a wheelbarrow, carted them outside, built a bonfire, and burned them. Another monk, horrified, gathered as many copies as possible of a different book, the *Graduale Romanum*, and hid them so they would be spared a similar fate. How many precious volumes, repositories of the wisdom and beauty of ages, were destroyed in this barbaric manner? "Vengeance is mine," says the Lord;[5] one can be certain that those who sinned against Catholic tradition have paid the last penny for it.

When I was being given a tour one October of a famous Benedictine monastery near Krakow, the young monk who was my guide stated outright that the younger monks wish to have the tabernacle back in the center, wish to celebrate Mass *ad orientem*, wish to recover Latin, and wish to receive communion kneeling and on the tongue, while their elders are opposed to all these things. This shift in desire is not merely "generational dynamics," as if we ought to expect the next generation to clamor for the opposite again—a Church forever ricocheting between chant scholas and folk bands, birettas and felt banners. No. The youth are awakening from the Rip van Winkle sleep of progressive liturgism—that weird coma between the ill-informed but thriving conservatism of the preconciliar age and the better-informed though struggling traditionalism of the postconciliar age.

We have heard and still hear a lot about the "charismatic movement," but no one can explain how in the world it is supposed to fit in with the Catholic Faith as it has matured and blossomed in the miracle-rich lives of the saints, full of ascetical sobriety and mystical transcendence, which are perfectly mirrored in the liturgical and

---

[4] Even Paul VI recognized this in the ill-starred apostolic letter *Sacrificium Laudis*, which insisted that retention of the Latin choral office would make the difference between attracting and repelling vocations.

[5] See Deut 32:35; Rom 12:19.

sacramental rites they knew and loved. What I have come to suspect, and what the contents of this book amply demonstrate, is that Traditionalism is the *real* charismatic movement in the Church today, and that it is high time we stop thwarting the Spirit. Would that today's shepherds and sheep would heed Gamaliel's hard-nosed advice:

> Ye men of Israel, take heed to yourselves what you intend to do, as touching these men. For before these days rose up Theodas, affirming himself to be somebody, to whom a number of men, about four hundred, joined themselves: who was slain; and all that believed him were scattered, and brought to nothing. After this man, rose up Judas of Galilee, in the days of the enrolling, and drew away the people after him: he also perished; and all, even as many as consented to him, were dispersed. And now, therefore, I say to you, refrain from these men, and let them alone; for if this council or this work be of men, it will come to nought; but if it be of God, you cannot overthrow it, lest perhaps you be found even to fight against God. (Act 5:35-39)

"If it be of God, you cannot overthrow it." No member of the body of Christ, high or low, can fight against God and win. The traditionalist movement is here to stay and is growing. Its adherents truly believe that the Eucharistic liturgy is the font and apex of the Christian life, and *act accordingly*. Those who oppose this movement are not just setting themselves up for failure, they are setting themselves up against the God who first bestowed the monuments of tradition on the Church, and then raised up a fitting attachment to them as powerful means of sanctification. The immemorial sacred liturgy as well as the desire of the people to worship God through it are *both* of the Holy Spirit. As we know, the sin against the Holy Ghost is the only sin that can never be forgiven, in this world or in the world to come.

I first noticed this return to tradition when I was a college student in the early 1990s in California. I noticed the same as a grad student in Washington, DC, in the mid-to-late '90s. I especially noticed it as a teacher of undergraduates and graduates from dozens of countries over the twenty-year period from 1998 to 2018—so many different countries and contexts, confirmed by so many additional correspondents, that I knew it was a genuinely worldwide awakening. The internet had something to do with it, to be sure, but primarily because it provided resources that *responded* to an already gnawing hunger for "something more" than flavorless pablum.

A decade ago, my son (then fifteen years old) and I participated in a Sacred Music Colloquium of the Church Music Association of America. As with the Sacra Liturgia conferences and many other such gatherings of which I've been a part, the participation was dominated by professionals, youths, and teens who unabashedly preferred the great music of our Catholic tradition, sacred in its stylistic qualities and well-suited to ritual. People from my generation (I was born in 1971) and younger *know*, without need for much explanation, that Gregorian chant, Renaissance polyphony, and post-Renaissance choral works of grand and intimate scale are the music of the Catholic liturgy.[6] Such music *says* "Catholic" the moment you hear it, which is why Hollywood always reaches for it when depicting anything Catholic. This vast repertoire, "a treasure of inestimable value, greater even than that of any other art,"[7] was written expressly for ecclesiastical ceremonies. At its best, it is not trying to compete with or emulate popular styles of music; it is not serving two masters; it is not a multi-purpose Swiss Army knife. It is *church* music, *sacred* music, pure and simple, and that is why it is so singularly effective and lovable. We admire what is pure and simple, because it fits its function to a T. It works. What isn't broken doesn't need to be fixed.

In a position paper written by the International Una Voce Federation, I once came across a phrase that struck me as an apt description of the two poles between which bad liturgy oscillates: Rationalism excludes silence and complex ceremonial, while Romanticism promotes informality and spontaneity. Rationalism and Romanticism—the two great counterforces of modernity, each an extreme in perpetual reaction against the other—are the two slave-drivers behind the liturgical reform.

Rationalism cracks the whip and shouts: "*No silence!* Everything must be SAID and UNDERSTOOD! No complexity! Stop all that intricate symbolic stuff! Stop all that lugubrious chanting! Modern

---

[6] The album *Benedicta* of the Monks of Norcia made it right to the top of the classical billboard, showing once again that the prayerful yearning for peace and transcendence expressed by Gregorian chant is not a passing fad but a constant need of our society. It would be helpful if prelates and pastors would pay attention to actual cultural trends like this one, instead of paying attention to what seemed to be trends several decades ago.

[7] Second Vatican Council, *Sacrosanctum Concilium* 112.

man has no patience, no time, no ability, no need for it! It promotes an aristocracy of clerics! Let the light of objective reason shine!" But then Romanticism sneaks in, elbows an unsuspecting Rationalism aside, and, with a voice all the more poisonous for its seeming amiability: "Relax! Go with the flow! You are too formal, uptight, rigid, and cerebral! Let go of the rubrics, find your inner child, feel it in your bones, *be yourself!* Everything's about YOU, your feelings, your neediness—this is *your moment!*" Each struggles for supremacy; in a weird sort of way, they are codependent and collaborative. They stop at nothing to eviscerate the tradition that precedes them, until all that is left is a disembodied reason of empty structures and a derationalized self-indulgent sentimentalism.

Be that as it may, what we see at work in the liturgical reform is a peculiarly self-centered assumption that the preoccupations of *modern Western man*—rationalism and romanticism being characteristic -isms of an imbalanced worldview and an inadequate philosophy—are the preoccupations of *all* of humanity, including Latin America, Africa, and Asia. As a result, the new liturgy is going to be imposed on every nation, every people, every culture, every generation, regardless of whether or not they meet the hyper-modern Eurocentric criteria on the basis of which it was designed. The absurdity of such an assumption is obvious, but it becomes even more obvious when one considers generational shifts.

It seems to me that just as there was a problem with assuming that African Catholics needed the new Mass when the old Mass under which they were evangelized was and still is, in fact, more suited to their temperament and culture,[8] there is an analogous problem with assuming that today's young Catholics, especially those who have been homeschooled or, at any rate, raised in a more traditional manner, or even those who have converted to Christ from indifference, worldliness, or hostility (we see them in these pages, too), automatically carry the same modernist or postmodernist burdens that the rest of Western society bears. Of course, we're all moderns in a host of subtle and obvious ways, but since a good deal of the

---

[8] See "Sub-Saharan Africa" in Joseph Shaw, ed., *The Case for Liturgical Restoration* (Brooklyn, NY: Angelico Press, 2019), 267–73; Peter Kwasniewski, "Mythbusting: 'African Catholicism is a Vatican II Success Story,'" *New Liturgical Movement*, January 23, 2023; A Nigerian Catholic, "Inculturation: A Wrong Turn," various dates, *New Liturgical Movement*, available https://drive.google.com/file/d/1Q2du4rMRBTwVpLUQQg20NsP3tccGkHD2/view.

modern mentality is a flight from reality and a sort of self-invited neurosis, it seems distinctly possible—and my decades of experience as a student and then as an undergraduate and graduate-level teacher have confirmed this over and over—that young people today might actually be *free* of a lot of the existential baggage of their elders. The problems of the sixties and seventies are just not the same as our problems. And young faithful Catholics have not necessarily *problematized* their existence, or the concept of tradition, or the concept of authority, or the concept of the sacred and the mystical.

We are still struggling with the fallout of Rationalism and Romanticism, but we are no longer (thanks be to God) as naïvely optimistic about the power of human reason or of sincere feelings to lead us into an Edenic new world of human brotherhood. It is too easy to be cynical at this point about such grandiose rhetoric. We are looking for something a lot more serious—something real and realistic, which, paradoxically, we sense will have to be very *different*, rather *strange* perhaps; something *transcendent*. Otherwise it is fake; it is looking at a mirror and falling in love with the image. We are looking for the original, the One from whom we come and to whom we are going.

At Sacra Liturgia, at the Colloquium, at all the schools I attended or worked for, I saw ample evidence that we are turning a corner. The rebels of the Age of Aquarius are pathetic and frail, and angry as hell (truly) that their revolution is crumbling before their very eyes, both for want of internal strength and for want of external interest. The youth who still want to practice their Faith need more, desire more, and deserve more than the Church's hierarchy has been willing (or even able?) to give them. And these young men and women, without much help from their superiors, are figuring out how to find their way back to the Tradition, in spite of all obstacles, detours, traps, and poor signage.

This movement—this hunger for Catholic Tradition—cannot be stopped. The testimonials found in these pages could be multiplied a hundredfold simply by traveling around to flourishing apostolates of the Priestly Fraternity of St. Peter, the Institute of Christ the King, the Society of St. Pius X, and diocesan TLMs and asking for submissions from the youth groups. But if the movement cannot be stopped, it *can* be either delayed by obstructionists who wish to earn burning coals or actively promoted by shepherds who care for the eternal destiny of their sheep. I am reminded in this connection of a butler's speech from a P. G. Wodehouse novel:

> It is my experience that opposition in matters of the 'eart is useless, feedin', as it so to speak does, the flame. Young people, your lordship, if I may be pardoned for employing the expression in the present case, are naturally romantic and if you keep 'em away from a thing they sit and pity themselves and want it all the more. And in the end you may be sure they get it. There's no way of stoppin' them.[9]

Indeed: the traditional movement is not going away. Meanwhile, our shepherds stand to gain glory or shame, depending on how they react to this impetus of the Holy Spirit. Let us pray for them daily.

The stakes are high. One wishes to say to our bishops: *Choose well*. To the youth (including the youthful clergy): Choose with discretion and courage, as did Samuel and Daniel, who, "though young, judged the elders."

---

[9] P. G. Wodehouse, *A Damsel in Distress*, Collector's Wodehouse (New York: Abrams, 2003), 238.

EDITOR'S INTRODUCTION

WHAT AN INCREDIBLE JOY AND HONOR IT HAS been to read the cornucopia of essays contained in this volume! The writings collected here represent the heartfelt and faith filled stories of young people across the world, from Africa, Europe, the Americas, and Asia. These contributions show just how accessible the Truth, Goodness, and Beauty of the Traditional Latin Mass are. They demonstrate the incredible transformations that the traditional Mass and traditional Catholic way of life enact upon young souls, especially those who come to the liturgy suffering from tepidity or who are initially resistant. Thank you to the many young people who have chosen to contribute to this book; you are proof that the gates of Hell shall not prevail, and that there is so much hope for the future of the Catholic faith! You are proof that, as Dr. Alice von Hildebrand said at the end of her life "In the end, God always wins."

As a scholar of Catholic liturgy, and one who specializes in studying musical & liturgical formation in modern Latin Mass communities, these essays have been eye opening and encouraging towards my research. Each of these reflections are a snapshot into living, breathing, and thriving communities of faith who are seeking God in one of the most beautiful ways imaginable: the Latin Mass. I hope that the readers of this volume, regardless of age, take inspiration from the voices speaking here, and come to love the Mass of the Ages as much as we do. I hope that those who are skeptical have their doubts assuaged and can approach the sublime and divine worship discussed here in a new way.

A note on the text itself. These essays were written by young people between the ages of 12 and 24 from all over the world. Consequently, they reflect a great diversity of skill and style in their composition: some essayists, for example, use American spelling while others used British; some capitalized words like "Mass" and "Rosary," while others chose not to, and so on. Rather than impose a uniform formatting, we chose to allow these editorial variants to stand in order to better reflect the individuality of each essayist. You may consequently notice differences in the use of spelling, numeration, capitalization, and italics throughout the book. This was an intentional editorial choice.

Finally, a few words of thanks are in order. A debt of gratitude is due to Dr. Peter Kwasniewski for his foreword, and his general support of the project. A few individuals were instrumental in promoting the project to help recruit essayists, notably Joe Lipa of Juventutem Michigan, Gregory DiPippo of New Liturgical Movement, and Alex Begin from the Detroit Latin Mass Community. Thanks to Allison Girone for graciously volunteering her lovely photography for the cover image, and to Jessica Fellmeth for the cover design. Special thanks as well to Cruachan Hill's intern Clare Weber for organizing the essays into a single manuscript, and to Michael Schrauzer for the typesetting. Finally, a special thanks to Phillip Campbell and Cruachan Hill Press for the opportunity to help support this project as an editor.

St. Gregory the Great, St. Pius V and St. Alphonsus Liguori, pray for us!

Reyers Phillip Brusoe
PhD Student University of Kentucky
August 2024

THE LATIN MASS AND THE YOUTH

1. UTTERLY FASCINATED
Duy, Age 21, Vietnam

Et in caritate perpetua dilexi te: ideo attraxi te, miserans.

"Yea I have loved thee with an everlasting love, therefore have I drawn thee, taking pity on thee" (Jer. 31:3)

ized T HE LATIN MASS HAS TOUCHED ME IN A QUIET and profound way, much like the way Jesus speaks or guides us from the depths of each person. I was born and raised in Vietnam, a country where there has been no precedent for celebrating the Latin Mass for the past 50 years, and all forms of liturgical celebrations follow the Novus Ordo. From the time of my baptism to my catechism classes at church, the Novus Ordo Mass was something that was always around me. I thought it was the way to pray and that I would be attached to it for the rest of my life.

But then one day, the unexpected finally happened. Since my parish still has a high altar according to the Extraordinary Form (in my country, most churches since the start of the Novus Ordo, have tended to eliminate everything related to the Tridentine Mass, including the high altar), I kept wondering why there was such an altar and it really attracted me in a way, as if God was making me find out and inviting me to this ancient form of liturgy. According to the introduction of an old priest in my parish, I found out that in addition to the Novus Ordo rite, there was also another form of rite that has existed for hundreds of years. I was very surprised to learn this! My journey started from there: I went on many different websites and learned about the TLM in more detail, but I understood very little of what I was reading. I started watching videos and looking at pictures, and I was utterly fascinated by the use of *ad orientem*, and all of the liturgical arts. Indeed, it was the first time I saw such beautiful things. At that time, I was only 16 years old. God guided me to find these things in such a wonderful way, I will never forget that for the rest of my life.

Time went by, until I met a few friends from online, and even more surprisingly, they were both fellow countrymen and supporters of the TLM. At that time, I was so excited because I couldn't believe this day would come. During that time, they told me and taught me a lot. Because we are fellow countrymen, the language barrier was no longer an obstacle to my passion for the traditional Latin Mass. The first gift I received from them was a handheld missal. My first impression of this gift was that it was really beautiful, the gold leaf patterns and the images at the beginning of each feast fascinated me, and I spent the whole night gazing at them. But sadly, I didn't know when to use it because there was no traditional Latin Mass at that time. I could only pray to God, asking him to give my country a priest to offer traditional Mass so that I could come and once experience this sacred and beautiful sacrifice at least once. I thought what I prayed to God was somewhat lofty and unlikely to happen because since the change to the new liturgical celebration, the TLM has no longer appeared on my country, and it has been over 50 years.

For over two years, I had been praying for a traditional Latin Mass to be celebrated in my country. To my surprise, one day, I received news that a foreign priest would be coming to teach at a monastery in my country. This priest was also a celebrant of the TLM, and he belonged to the Priestly Fraternity of St. Peter (FSSP). After completing his teaching, he decided to establish a community in my country. Thus, after more than 50 years, the Traditional Latin Mass had finally returned to my homeland.

The first time I attended this Mass, everything was so sacred and solemn. The incense smoke that filled the air made me feel like I was in heaven. Every gesture and action were meticulous and careful. After the Mass, I approached him, and he explained that every action he performed during the Mass represented a step in the process from when Jesus instituted the Eucharist to when he died on the Cross. I couldn't believe that the Traditional Latin Mass held so much meaning.

To further satisfy my undying passion for this Mass, I decided to ask the priest to allow me to join the altar server team at the community he oversaw. The first time I served Mass, I was a bit nervous because I didn't know how to respond, and I was afraid that I wouldn't be able to keep up with the priest's gestures. However, the priest seemed to know this, and he guided me through everything before I served Mass for the first time. I prepared for this for over a week, even though the first Mass I served was a Low Mass. Being closer to the altar, I was able to observe the priest's every action more closely and assist with tasks in the sacristy, which gave me a deeper understanding of this sacred liturgy. God answered my prayers more than I could have imagined, "Quam magnificata sunt opera tua, Domine!" — "How great are thy works, O Lord!" (Ps.103)

To this day, I serve at TLM every day and I have been intimately attached to it for over five years now. God has helped me discover a more vibrant way of living out the Tridentine rite and almost forgotten sacred arts. I wonder if it hadn't been for that old priest telling me about the Traditional Latin Mass, would I even know about it now? Praise be to God for ever watching over me every day of my life, and for setting my heart on fire with love for Him through this beautiful, venerable, and holy liturgical celebration, which is a more noble and honourable than ever before.

2. BEAUTY REDISCOVERED
Jay, Age 23, Philippines

AS I APPROACH MY 23RD YEAR IN 2024, REMIniscing about my journey into attending the Traditional Latin Mass fills me with gratitude for the decision I made. Growing up in a Catholic household in the Philippines, our practice was not as devout as some. While we observed significant liturgical celebrations like Ash Wednesday, Palm Sunday, and Christmas Eve, regular attendance at Mass was not a strict routine. My understanding of the faith remained superficial, limited to what I learned in elementary school, and my practice was more out of obligation than conviction.

Upon returning to our rural province in Nueva Ecija with my mother, I became involved in the youth ministry at our parish. Encouraged by a relative to join and make new friends, I found myself gradually immersed in the activities, including participation in the parish choir, and attending Sunday Masses. However, the Mass experiences of my teenage years were characterized by liturgical dancing, lay ministers leading the Mass, and a style of worship heavily influenced by Protestant practices. While initially engaging, this approach failed to foster a deeper connection to my Catholic faith.

I witnessed many of my peers and fellow youth ministry members drift away from the Church in search of a more spiritually fulfilling experience elsewhere, and I began to question my own beliefs. Amidst the allure of other denominations promising inner peace, I grappled with doubts about the authenticity of my faith. It was a period of uncertainty and contemplation, marked by a sense of detachment from my Catholic identity.

Despite these lingering doubts, I continued to attend Mass, more as a gesture to please my family than out of genuine conviction. It wasn't until my senior year of high school when I joined a Catholic apologetics group that I began to delve deeper into my faith. While I gained valuable knowledge and insights from this experience, I still struggled to reconcile my doubts with the contemporary celebration of the Mass.

Amidst conflicting opinions within the group regarding the merits of the Latin Mass, I encountered a stranger on Facebook who intrigued me with discussions about its significance. I was sceptical yet curious, so I embarked on a journey of discovery, seeking to understand the roots of the current crisis in the Church and the appeal of the Tridentine Mass, especially to young people who were my age. Despite encountering resistance from some within my apologetics group who dismissed the Latin Mass as antiquated and irrelevant, I persisted in my quest for truth.

Through online research and discussions with newfound friends, I gained a deeper appreciation for the solemnity and reverence of the Traditional Latin Mass and the present crisis of the Church today. The beauty and the sense of awe it inspired in me were unlike anything I had experienced before. I attended my first Latin Mass in Pampanga. It opened my eyes to a form of worship that resonated deeply with my spiritual longing and journey to find inner peace.

Further exploration and curiosity led me to Archbishop Marcel Lefebvre's "Open Letter to Confused Catholics," which shed light on the crisis facing the Church and the importance of preserving tradition. I was invited to attend the Latin Mass at Our Lady of Victories Church, run by the Society of St. Pius X, in Quezon City. I was moved to tears by the profound sense of reverence and devotion I experienced especially when the priest lifted the Sacred Host. Like St. Thomas, who doubted the Resurrection of Our Lord, I too exclaimed, "My Lord and my God!" when I received Him in Holy Communion.

The Traditional Latin Mass has been instrumental in deepening my understanding of my faith. It is the same Mass attended by the saints, making it the most venerable rite in Christendom. It is the Mass our ancestors turned to for spiritual nourishment, brought to our islands by missionaries. It is the Mass for which many saints and martyrs gave their lives to defend. Now, after almost five years of attending the Latin Mass, it continues to enrich my spiritual journey.

The Traditional Latin Mass has since become the cornerstone of my spiritual life. I regularly attend Confession, study traditional catechisms, and serve as an altar server in the Archconfraternity of St. Stephen. It has deepened my appreciation for the richness of my faith and connected me to the Church's timeless traditions.

In the words of Cardinal Newman, "I could attend Mass forever, and not be tired." My journey to the Traditional Latin Mass has reignited my love for the beauty and solemnity of our Catholic heritage. It is my hope that more Catholics will rediscover the profound richness of this ancient liturgical tradition and embrace it as a source of spiritual nourishment and renewal.

3. A NITTY-GRITTY TRAD
John Paul, Age 18, North Dakota

I'VE BEEN GOING TO MASS EVER SINCE I WAS four. For the first nine years that I went to Mass, it was at my local suburban Novus Ordo parish. Pretty typical. Nothing traditional, but nothing too crazy. You had your Extraordinary Ministers, your lay lectors and whatnot, but usually none of the guitar blessings or other such shenanigans. I was fine with it, really. I did my best to engage with it, following along with the readings and the breaking of the eucharistic bread. It was nice when Holy Week came around. Even with all that, though, I was never really impacted deeply. If you could take it all away, I'd be more-or-less the same person.

My first experience of the Latin Mass that I recall was receiving my First Communion at the FSSP parish we currently attend. They had catechism after one of the Saturday morning Masses, so we'd make our way up there for Low Mass and then class. If I am being honest, though, I didn't really notice how different the traditional Mass was at first. At this point, I had experienced many other churches aside from the one I regularly attended on Sundays; I was used to the liturgy varying from church to church. The only thing I remember noticing and thinking was cool was the genuflection during the Last Gospel. It was because everyone would genuflect, and then just a couple of seconds later, everyone would kneel for the Leonine prayers. Genuflecting outside of the context of entering the pew was new to me, I suppose.

Anyways, I went on to receive my First Holy Communion in the TLM. Apparently, it was a Solemn High Mass, though I don't really remember noticing any of that. I only remember Father saying in his sermon something along the lines of "just because you're done now doesn't mean you should forget everything you learned," and also being very happy to have received Our Lord. Well, after that I stopped regularly going to Latin Mass for quite some time. I guess I didn't listen to Father, as I almost immediately stopped receiving on the tongue and went back to receiving on the hand. I mean, what can I say? I was just an impressionable kid. It was what everyone else did. I shudder thinking about it now.

About five years later, in 2019, it came time for me to do Confirmation. By this point, my Novus Ordo parish had shifted from doing catechesis on Saturdays to doing it on Sundays, which meant that it conflicted with the family going to the local church. My parents provided the music for the Sunday 10 AM Mass at our local parish, which meant that they had to be present for that particular liturgy. So, my brother and I (who did Confirmation) would carpool up with friends and go to the Latin High Mass, and then Confirmation class. That was when things started changing for me, though I didn't realize it so much at the time. For one thing, I started going to confession more often. Prior, I only went twice a year, at the penance services my church held before Christmas and Easter. And in general, my Catholic Faith started becoming a lot more important to me. My parents had done a good job of planting lots of Catholic "seeds" in me, but I don't think they really started developing much until this point.

At this point, I had already joined the parish Altar Guild (e.g., Mass servers). I had actually joined in late 2018 but would only go up to the monthly meetings and then not really be that involved. Eventually, I started going to Low Mass occasionally with friends and training a little bit more seriously, but not much. Despite being trained many times, it was a long time before I ended up serving Low Mass. I was just thrust into it by the guy. He was like, "I think you're ready." And I was like, "okay." I knew my responses but that was about it . . . it was a disaster. I learned a lot about making mistakes and how to move on from them and learn from them. And also I learned to take corrections; I took a liking to Proverbs 12:1: "He that loveth correction, loveth knowledge: but he that hateth reproof is foolish."

In 2020 everything halted due to COVID. My confirmation class was stopped. My parish stopped having public Mass (though the church doors were only locked for the live stream Masses and we never stopped having confessions). That wasn't very shocking at first. I just figured it was normal for society to shut down and stop everything owing to disease; I didn't question it. But after the two weeks started getting expanded, I started getting depressed.

Eventually, though, things happened and we started getting to Mass at my parish again, so I stopped being depressed. Ah, I said we. At this point, my whole family started going to Mass at the TLM, not just me and my brother. This was because my parents didn't have to do music for the local parish anymore owing to Covid. Going to Mass again made me really thankful, and that's when things REALLY took off. I got good at serving Mass—after all, we had five Low Masses on weekdays, and eight on Sundays, so I was doing it almost every day. I also joined the music program, even though my parish wasn't having Sung Mass yet.

Our parish life went through a lot of shifts, each one more and more pleasant, until we've now reached something that's pretty normal. I'm pretty much a trad now. A nitty-gritty trad, having become acquainted with the inner workings of the liturgy. I've become an accomplished altar boy and an accomplished member of the choir. I've made lots and lots of friends. Indeed, my church is my social life. But yeah. I've got a LOT to be thankful for. No way I'm gonna be able to make it up to God, but I can sure as heck try.

4. TRUTH, GOODNESS, AND BEAUTY
Fred, Age 19, Michigan

LEX ORANDI, LEX CREDENDI, LEX VIVENDI. Translated loosely from the Latin, the preceding phrase means roughly "the law of prayer, which is the law of belief, becomes the law of life." While popularized by Pope Benedict XVI, this phrase can be traced all the way back to St. Vincent of Lérins, a Gallic monk from the fifth century. The phrase provides an important formulation for believers, as it enables them to grasp more fully the transcendental and individual implications of the Truth, Beauty, and Goodness present in the *Usus Antiqiuor* of the Roman Catholic Church.

As a Catholic, I am privileged to see the transcendent elements in this most sacred Liturgy, this summary of Catholic worship and belief. Furthermore, I have been individually blessed by Almighty God through this transformative experience which has brought me to a place better than I would have ever thought possible.

Before I first experienced these elements of Truth, Goodness, and Beauty in the Liturgy, I was not fit to be called a Christian. I did not practice the faith of my ancestors interiorly. I went through the motions, but my Catholic faith was just a superficial identity. That all changed when I first experienced the *Usus Antiquior*. Now, no longer was I a disinterested observer at a banal religious experience. I had, for once, a strong experience of an objectively sacred structure. The ancient language, the soaring melodies, and glory of architecture, vesture, and proportion was an astounding thing for me to behold.

One might object that the reaction I had was merely a subjective response to an impressive experience. Perhaps this is a part of it. Such a response, however, fails to illustrate the full implications of the matter. Plenty of people are astounded and awed by elements such as these, either individually or collectively. Yet, how many change their lives because of that experience? How many times does one walk into a theatre house, a concert hall, or a museum, and decide that one's life must be transfigured because of what one experiences inside there?

Encounters with Truth and Beauty have a transformative capability associated with them, insofar as they comprise elements within the law of prayer: ritual, response, and of course, sacrifice — all the aspects of this law have the transcendentals as key elements which define them. The *Usus Antiquior* of the Roman Rite, imbued as it is with Truth, Goodness, and Beauty, has had a deeply transformative effect upon me, personally speaking. From the place I described earlier, of having little interior belief, I resolved that my life should mirror the worship which I love so dearly.

It has not been a simple, swift, or painless process. But when it becomes wearying, as any constant path is like to become from time to time, it is then that our Lord's words ring the truer to me: "If any man will come after me, let him deny himself, and *take up his cross.*" A cross is not always comfortable, nor always appreciated, but it remains constant. Despite our attitudes, it continues to be one thing: an instrument of our sanctification. And in an age where many think any proposition inherently subjective, a constant is a thing of Truth and a thing of Beauty.

In conclusion, I would not be the man I am now, but for the grace of God and the experience of the Latin Mass. The experience of an especial Truth and Beauty in this law of prayer has truly become the law of my belief. This in turn has become the law of my life, shaping me into a "new creation of Christ," as St. Paul says. For this, I am grateful to the Almighty. Truly I can now say, with the poet Keats, that "Truth is Beauty and Beauty Truth, that is all ye know on earth, and all ye need to know."

5. LIKE FALLING IN LOVE
Marius, Age 23, South Carolina

MANY RECOGNIZE THE UNMATCHED BEAUTY, character, mystery, and value of the Latin Mass. This is usually first known through the senses: the chant, the incense, the sacred vestments. This is also the way the Latin Mass first attracted me. Over time, these aesthetics unmistakably pointed and guided me to the heart of the Mass: the sacrifice of calvary. In other words, something subjective (to a degree) led me to something objective. I would like to briefly share my discovery of the Latin Mass with the hope that others will be drawn in as I have been.

I first encountered the Latin Mass as a young child. Early on, I got the impression that traditional Catholics were not the crowd I was supposed to be around. The rest of my youth I spent at a Novus Ordo parish that preserved and cultivated the sacred arts to the best of its ability. This was my first exposure to sacred music, reverent worship, and inspiring clerical piety. Yet, I was never at peace, and I sensed that something was missing. I was an altar server my whole youth, with a keen sense for the sacred—no matter how much I desired it, the Novus Ordo did not fill my cup.

By God's providence, I ended up at one of the finest liberal arts institutions in the states—Thomas Aquinas College—where I was instilled with a desire for the Good, the True, and the Beautiful. It is during this time that I fell in love with the Latin Mass. Reflecting on my time at Thomas Aquinas, I realize that my studies prepared me to recognize the beauty of the Latin Mass like nothing else. It is clear to me that reading the greatest works of Western Civilization would dispose me to seeing its source and summit. My first attraction was similar to the way a man falls in love with a woman. I loved the chant, the incense, the suit and tie on Sundays, and the new personal missal. This new and ancient liturgy fascinated and excited me greatly. I loved it to the degree that I thought I was called to the religious life, which lead me to monasteries in Clear Creek, Oklahoma, and Norcia, Italy.

Over time, I have been able to articulate a few reasons why the Latin Mass attracts me. The first reason is the sacred aesthetics: The Latin (sacred language), the elaborate vestments (sacred superfluity),

Gregorian chant (sacred music). They are common human things that we have set aside for the sole purpose of worship. This continually reassures me that the Mass is what it claims to be, and that God really is the Being that deserves the purest, most noble sacrifice. The sacredness and exclusivity of the use of the liturgical instruments reminds me that I myself must set aside the best that I have as an offering to God.

Mother Church also is *Magistra*. Through the Liturgy, and all the sacred arts that are present in it, Mother Church is teaching us essential truths about the Faith. The Latin Mass has imposed certain things upon me that make me *freer* to love God. For example: It is required that I receive our Lord on the tongue, and if possible, kneeling down. If I practice receiving our Lord in the most reverent way, I will more deeply believe that Jesus is truly present in the Eucharist: there is a conformity between my beliefs and my actions. There seems to be great conformity between the Faith and the Latin Mass in more than this aspect. It is also customary to bow to the celebrant when he enters and exits the church. It took me a while to see the significance of this. Who is the priest? He is *in persona Christi*. Bowing to the priest reminds me of the sacred office and of his special and noble calling. Ultimately, this act of reverence deepens my love of our Lord, and it makes me more conscious of Jesus' presence in the Mass.

All these aspects of the Latin Mass reinforce my awareness of the deeper *reality* present. What are all these sacred arts pointing to? What is their end? My first experience was that these things simply raised my mind to God. This is still the case to this day. When I smell incense or hear Gregorian Chant, my mind is immediately raised to God. In themselves, the aesthetics point me to God, and lead me to an awareness of the deeper reality present at Mass. What is the deeper reality? It is the sacrifice on Calvary being made present on the altar. From this sacrifice, communion necessarily flows. The Latin Mass has made clear to me that the sacrifice is the heart of the Mass, and our participation, or our *communion*, is the necessary consequence, similar to an essential attribute. It has informed my understanding of my relationship to my neighbor: I love him through Jesus. What unites me with the stranger sitting next to me at Mass? It is the Sacrifice. In this world, it is only in virtue of the sacrifice that we can be united with Christ in His mystical body. In a sense, I have experienced a Copernican revolution in worship. Most of my life I had the impression that Mass was primally an act of the community — even my personal act. The Latin Mass has shown me that it is only *my* action or the action of the *community* insofar as it is united to Christ's act. This awareness has increased my sense that Mass is the greatest form of worship. Is it not staggering that we are allowed to participate in the Son's act of obedience to the Father?

I think the Latin Mass is something Mother Church has lovingly preserved and developed over the ages for me. It is a spiritual gift — a spiritual treasure chest — that my Lord has left *me*. Guided by the Holy Spirit, and made manifest in tradition, the Church is able to teach us the best way to worship. I am often filled with a sense of awe when I go to the Latin Mass: the sacred superfluity, the clearness of its actions, the dedication of its congregation. As I mature in age and wander through life as a pilgrim, the Latin Mass is a source of peace, clarity, strength, and consolation. *Deo gratias!*

6. THE INCOMPARABLE BEAUTY OF THE TRADITIONAL LITURGY'S MUSIC
Elijah, Age 18, Wisconsin

I'M A MUSIC COMPOSER. THE TRADITIONAL Latin Mass is the uncontested greatest inspiration for my desire to experience, cultivate, and create beautiful liturgical music. One line in St. Augustine's *Confessions* succinctly summarizes my history with sacred music and the Latin Mass: "Late have I loved Thee; O Beauty ever ancient, ever new!"

Five years ago, when our family moved from Michigan to Wisconsin, neither subject could have been of lesser interest to me. Growing up, the words "Christian" and "music" put together indicated little more than summer bible school sing-alongs and the dull hand motions engineered to score youth crowd engagement with those songs; the dates of our available selection of church hymns ranged from about the 1960s to the 1970s; Latin itself was an alien concept. What "interest" was there to have?

Although I never expected a higher standard of liturgical beauty other than that which I received as a kid, upon moving, our family curiously began attending the Traditional Latin Mass, the only one we had ever had available near home. We first attended hesitantly once a month; that became every other week, loosely holding on by alternating Sundays with the closer-by English parish, where we had made more friends anyways; then we finally committed to the Latin Mass every Sunday. The transition was neither seamless nor easy. I lost frequency not only with new friends and what little familiarity we had just gained in this new home, but also with my own native English tongue–a line not previously crossed (even as we crossed the state border line as strangers in this strange land).

However, while managing this rough transition, one temperate summer morning at an Extraordinary Form Pontifical High Mass, as the congregation prepared to receive Holy Communion, began the choir's intonation of the finest work my ears had heard that I did not even comprehend as possible in a Catholic liturgy: Franz Biebl's *Ave Maria*.

"Angelus Domini nuntiavit Mariae, et concepit de Spiritu Sancto."
*"The Angel of the Lord declared unto Mary,
and she conceived of the Holy Spirit."*

Those simple notes, and the piece that followed, resonated within me more fiercely than any other before. It did not merely perk my ears or incline my attention, as a song on the radio or at a theme park would. The piece animated a new desire that I carried up the aisle and back down while also carrying the True Presence within me. The desire was not just to hear beautiful music, but to *make* beautiful music–something which, to me, was just as alien as the language the piece was sung in. Needless to say, when we truly settled in Wisconsin, summer bible school and the 1970s hymnal selections stayed far behind. What has stayed with me is what I sought and continue to seek: To bring communities together and to draw souls closer to Christ with music that adorns our liturgies as mosaics adorn our altars and cathedrals. In the past year alone, my choral music has been performed in concerts, theater productions, and above all, at the Latin Mass. Every day I get the opportunity to cherish, cultivate, and challenge myself with the music that glorifies God, unites the Christian faithful, and which I have fervently pursued: that same beauty, ever ancient and ever new.

Sacred music in the Traditional Latin Mass not only underscores the ancient, traditional beauty of the Church but also the timeless, universal nature with which the Church was established by Christ's own intention. "And not for them only do I pray, but for them also who through their word shall believe in me; That they all may be one, as thou, Father, in me, and I in thee; that they also may be one in us; that the world may believe that thou hast sent me" (John 17:20-21, Douay-Rheims).

The Latin Mass is universal as the Church is universal. When the priest sings the Exultet at the Easter Vigil Mass, those same notes and words echo worldwide with every other celebrant or concelebrant who sings them. The *Victimae Paschali Laudes* on Easter Sunday, proclaiming the triumph of the resurrected Christ, is not only sung by each choir in each Latin Mass parish in the world, but they are singing as one, all proclaiming the Sacrifice of the Lamb and the salvation of the world together. When the sequence of the *Veni Sancte Spiritus* is sung on Pentecost Sunday, it is not my fifteen-person choir in Wisconsin but the singular voice of the Church praying for the comfort and the gifts of the Holy Ghost upon us all. Likewise, on Good Friday when the priest exits the darkened church in silence, the whole Church stands in silence. The Church mourns together. The Church rejoices together. The Church sings together. The Church worships together. The whole Church is one, and over the years I have been astounded to unravel the truth that no liturgy emphasizes this more fully than the Traditional Latin Mass.

Like the Mass, sacred music is not only about bending towards engagement with the youth, although it has certainly engaged me, and the thousands of other young Catholics drawn to the Latin Mass yearly. It is not about appealing to any particular time in history, nor is it just white noise to stimulate the noisy mind of the layperson. It is, in fact, starkly different from the world because Christ has called us out of the world, and nowhere have I found this holy unworldliness better than the Traditional Latin Mass. The point of sacred music is to worship Christ as one; the point of striving for excellence in sacred music is to worship Christ more fully. As music itself is the handmaiden of the liturgy, so too is the full breadth of Catholic liturgical music–all centuries included–the handmaiden of the liturgy of the Traditional Latin Mass. The Latin Mass's music offers itself as an instrument for us to direct our worship to something much higher; it demands a solemnity and gravity for which the Holy Mass ought to be prayed simply because it is the Holy Mass.

Although I was initially reluctant to attend it, the Traditional Latin Mass has offered me something more precious than familiarity. It is a prayer more worth striving for than any other prayer, a voice clearer to me than my native English tongue, a home more resemblant to my heavenly home than any other, and a worship truly worth bringing to others–even outsiders and complete strangers — to the Gospel of Christ. It could not be more relevant to our time, especially to those in my generation, many of whom have grown up darkened to the knowledge of Christ and to the beauty of His universal, unconditional Love, and who might just discover the deepness of that Love through the beauty, mystery, and unworldliness of the Latin Mass. Through every page of sacred music I write, I wish only to emphasize that which the Traditional Latin Mass is a universal answer to the universal call to holiness, the timeless response of the faithful to Christ's endless Love, and an extraordinary form of worship that challenges each person involved to worship and give of themselves even more fully.

7. SEEKING THE GIFTS OF THE LORD
Carlo, Age 24, Panama

It was the second time I attended Mass for Septuagesima. My friends and I woke up early before dawn for the forty-five-minute drive, picking up a few others along the way. Mass started at 7:30 AM. This was the first time we drove to a high Mass since the new year, and although I would have liked to do it every week, the starting time for the long drive made consistency difficult for our rag-tag group of college students. As we entered the church, the warm light inside seemed to dispel the outer gloom. Despite the time, the parish was full of people, young and old, and many families with young children. As I said my prayers before Mass, trying to shake off the sleepiness, my attention was drawn to the arching golden letters above the apse that read *Exurgens autem Joseph a somno*, and Joseph awoke from sleep. There was comfort in those words, a sense of solidarity with the foster father of Christ. The bell rang, and the organ started with the procession. It was my senior year of college, and I would be soon leaving the state for unknown places; despite the uncertain future I was facing, I was at peace knowing that wherever I went, I would be home in the ancient liturgy.

I was born and raised in Panama, where I lived until I left for college. The land of my youth resembled Christendom in many ways, but it was lacking in one key aspect: it had lost its spirit. I do not mean that every Panamanian is an apostate; far from it, there are many there who are rich in the life of grace. But the Church and her rites do not occupy the same place in people's lives as they once did. A slow erosion of morality has taken place in the older generations, especially seen through corruption and loss of family values; lacking their example, younger people are more susceptible to the allurements of the world. As a whole, society has lost the animating spirit behind the principles that bind it together, and while it outwardly remains Christian, there is little left to anchor it down to the truths of the faith on which it was founded.

From a young age, I learned to follow the precepts of the Church, and to generally try to be a good person. Despite the best efforts of my family and catechists, like many in my generation I found very little interest and satisfaction in the Christian life. Like my peers, I found

Church teaching antiquated and unfit for the modern world. Part of it was that I was not aware of the Old Rite, and assumed that given the lack of alternatives, the corny liturgies of my youth were the historical norm for the Church, with their 70's music and strong Panamanian folk influences. Participating in the Mass required saying the responses, clapping during the songs, and shaking everyone's hand at the sign of peace. To me, being Catholic meant going to Mass every Sunday and holy day of obligation, going to confession twice a year, and receiving Our Lord in Holy Communion a few more times than that. Over time, I developed a sense that that was normal and sufficient.

Although the *aggiornamento* of the 1970s had been thorough, there were visible remnants of the old order still present, both physically and culturally. High altars were always a mystery to me because I had never seen one being used, yet the ones that remained felt more central to the sanctuary than the freestanding altars where Mass was celebrated. One story that is deeply engrained in the Panamanian identity is that of the *Altar de Oro*, the golden altar, which adorns the church of San José, in Panama City. This magnificent altar used to be covered in gold, and of great fame. As the legend goes, when Panama was sacked by pirates in 1671, the priests hid it by covering it in pitch, and pretending it was not finished so the pirates would not destroy it to steal the gold. Whenever I saw the altar, I was always confused by the existence of something so valuable that served as no more than the backdrop of the liturgy. Not even the gilded tabernacle within it remains in use since most churches in Panama store the Blessed Sacrament in a separate chapel.

The society I lived in, even though outwardly Catholic, did not hint to the deeper richness of the faith in ways I could understand. This was not because I was not sufficiently catechized, but because the liturgy, that which is supposed to be the highest and most sublime, home to the source and summit of the spiritual life, was in practice as not much more than a social exercise. I did not know that there was more to the Catholicism. That was the conclusion I arrived at from the disordered emphasis on the communal aspect of the Mass, homilies focused on social issues, and a general lackadaisical attitude from all involved. The Mass as the unbloody representation of the sacrifice of Calvary was something I had heard, and assented to intellectually, but it was not a lived reality. My liturgical experience taught me that spiritual matters were something to be accepted intellectually but did not need to be strictly observed.

Through the unexpected guidance of providence, I eventually found myself in the United States attending Oregon State University. Encountering the Catholic community there led to my first reversion, as the witness of others my age who took their faith seriously, and the fruit that it bore in their lives, clued me into the fact that there was more to Christianity than I originally thought. The missionary priestly society who ministered to the university were not traditionalists but labored faithfully and fruitfully. This novel discovery prompted an intellectual conversion and a desire to engage seriously with my beliefs. I wanted to live the same joy as those around me.

Experiencing the faith in the U. S. showed me another form of rupture that I had not witnessed back home: that of the themed Masses. By this I mean Masses that vary the music or the *ars celebrandi* to cater to a particular group: Masses with 70's hymns for those who preferred that, contemporary Masses with modern music to cater to the youth, and Spanish Masses for the Hispanic communities. As someone who identified with the latter two groups, I found the separation between peoples a bit disheartening, and it felt like the natural result of a ritual that should have brought them together. Once more, I could not relate the experience of what I had seen to the universal faith that overcame tribal boundaries and evangelized the New World.

I felt a strong conviction that the Lord wanted me to act for the unity of these groups. Now, consciously for the first time I wanted to know "How did we get here?" If there was division, it was crucial to me to know whence it stemmed, not merely as an intellectual reality, but also a historical one. At a more personal level, situating myself within the bigger narrative of salvation history seemed like a necessary foundation to honor my parents and their culture as a stranger in a foreign land. With my newfound confidence stemming from the witness of my friends, I started investigating into these issues, and I noticed that there was something profoundly different between my experience of the faith and that of prior generations, something that could not be accounted for merely by the technological peculiarities of modernity. I became aware of the deep changes that took place after the Council. Through the help of a roommate, I read much about the Latin Mass, yet I could not comprehend it. I only understood what it was not, and its mystery made me desire it even more.

My first encounter with old Mass was not grand or shocking, yet it was still richer and more profound than I ever imagined. It was a gloomy Monday evening in the middle of January; a couple roommates and I decided to drive one hour to visit a small-town parish where the TLM was being offered. As we sat on the pews in the cold and nearly empty wooden church, in the ethereal silence of a Low Mass, I realized I had found what I was looking for. This was the key that I was missing to finally understand the world that surrounded me, and the meaning of true religion. I could surrender myself whole-heartedly to it because it was coherent and at peace with itself. No longer were the two altars fighting for dominance in the sanctuary, nor the priest and the cross fighting for attention. The abstract theological formulae of my youth gave way to the concrete knowledge of an incarnate truth: I had been transported to Calvary, where Christ, drawing all things to himself, made the world whole again.

The priest, joyful at the presence of unknown young faces, cordially invited us to return on Septuagesima a couple weeks later. This was a Sunday I had read about in rubrics before, but I knew little about it other than its existence. That evening we arrived late at home, tired from the drive, but at the same time stirred up with apostolic fervor. We knew we had to invite all our friend group to join us on our next visit. It was the first High Mass at that parish since the reforms of the seventies, but it was excellently put together. I could feel the richness of meaning that was present in every action and word, even though I could not understand it. Looking around, I could witness that lost unity that I had been longing for, young and old people of diverse backgrounds worshipping together through a single rite.

I realize that the reverence that drew me to the Latin Mass might seem like the result of superficial details, which can be incorporated into reverent celebrations of the New Mass, but there is more to it than that. I find that the ancient and methodical movements of the Mass provide an alternative way of life that is antithetical to the constant stimulation of modernity. The arcane obscurity of its origins helps me enter into the mystery of the Divine Providence, which orders all things for the glory of Christ. Every year, as I go through the liturgical cycle, I look forward to the same familiar chants and readings; every year, I look forward to the coming of Septuagesima, and the call of St. Paul to strive for the hope of an imperishable crown.

8. "IN THE PRESENCE OF GOD!"
Maria Felicitas, Age 22, Nigeria

MY NAME IS MARIA FELICITAS AND I'LL BE writing about my discovery of the Traditional Latin Mass and how it has impacted and indeed changed my life in a beautiful way. My journey to the TLM began way before I can remember. I've always had knowledge of the TLM, although it was distorted. While growing up my mom used to tell us and warn us against the errors common in the new mass, things like receiving Our Lord in the hand or receiving Him while standing and how wrong they are. She told us about this Old Mass we thought was just the Latin of the new mass and was old-fashioned. She'll tell us about how as a little kid they were taught in their Eucharist Crusaders class how the smoke of the devil had entered the church and how the prayer to St Michael was composed. She never attended the old Mass herself as she was born just around the time the TLM was banned. But they believed in the teachings of this ancient Mass of the church.

To a large extent, my siblings and I didn't comprehend what was so wrong with the changes. Now I realize that our heads had been filled with many lies, which is why I was so awed by the truth when I found it in the TLM. A few years before I left for university, I made inquiries as to where the Latin Mass was being said in the state but was told the priest had travelled out of the country and there was no one to continue. Fast forward to 2023 when I finally entered university in August and a month later, I heard about a group of Catholic students, members of Mary Queen of All Hearts Confraternity in the Federal University of Technology in Owerri. These students drive over 60 miles and back to attend the Latin Mass every Sunday. It was first out of curiosity that I wanted to attend, to see this Mass that my mom told us so much about and to know what so attracted students to spend so much time and so much money to attend it.

On Sunday, September 24, I attended the traditional Latin Mass for the first time. What first struck me when we finally got to the parish was how beautiful the environment looked, the flowers, and the neatness and quietness. This is something that is not common in a country like Nigeria. Everything was entirely new to me. From the beautiful holy pictures and sculptures around the church, to the design and beauty of the altar, the gorgeous flowers on the altar, how everyone was seated and composed, and the large amount of old people present. *Everything* was screaming "In the presence of God!" The Mass started and I heard Gregorian chant for the first time or maybe not the first time, but this time struck me. Hearing them chant the entrance hymn I could only imagine what hearing the angels sing and being in heaven would feel like.

At the end of the mass, I had a bunch of questions and there was this inner peace I felt. It was just so beautiful and solemn, especially during the consecration: it depicted Calvary in full. There was a lot of discovery afterward I was so thrilled, I felt I had been deprived all my life. I just wanted to tell everyone just like how the Samaritan woman went about telling everyone she had found the Christ. A few weeks later I was consecrated and received the brown scapular of Our Lady of Mount Carmel.

I used to think of myself as a devoted Catholic and someone who knew the faith well. I thought I had charity, I thought I was doing God's will. And all I could utter after each picture catechism class after the second Mass was "Why haven't I known this all my life, why is this truth hidden and despised?" Then I discovered how the traditional catholic community lives, dresses, and sees God in everything. The love I felt for the Mass was spontaneous and I got comments like "Why don't you question these teachings you just accept everything?" and I would respond "It's what the saints believed in, so I believe too."

I started watching documentaries on the mass and listening to sermons on websites like Sensus Fidelium and Regina Prophetarum. A friend had asked if I see myself becoming a traditional Catholic and I had responded I can't see myself leaving the life I've known all my life but now it's the word of Our Lord to the rich man in Matthew 19:21-24 saying to me just as St Anthony of Padua said to the rich man "THERE CAN NEVER BE AN END UNTIL THERE'S A BEGINNING." I can say it is the Blessed Virgin drawing me closer to her son through this means to be Catholic. Ave Maria!

My knowledge of the saints grew, and I started reading a lot of spiritual books. I saw how important it is for me to save my soul and how little time I had left. I had this inner happiness each time after the Mass, and I just want to sit for long hours after mass in silence before the altar of God. It was something I had never felt before and this feeling and beauty is ever new each time. I was seeing the Catholic faith in the way the saints described it. I saw how I needed to take up my cross and follow him and not to go after the things of the world. I lack the words to describe my discovery and how it has affected me both spiritually and morally.

In the TLM I see an active church: The Church Militant, the Church Triumphant and the Church Suffering. The TLM changed my way of praying from asking for vain things to ask to love God. It gave me a deep understanding of the importance of the sacraments. In every sermon I heard a call to repentance and not how God has carried all my sorrows as is preached in churches these days. It was something that struck me, the huge difference in the homilies. I am used to hearing how God will bless us with wealth like King Solomon and everybody went to church because of what they want God to do for them. But it was a different spirituality I found in the TLM. I saw how the mothers are not busy building careers but taking care of their homes and raising Godly children.

Each day I found a new truth about the faith. The beauty in nature, the beauty in being skillful, the beauty in modesty. I saw Catholicism in a way I've never seen it before. The ancient architectural buildings, the ancient hymns, the ancient way of worship and everything so beautiful and ever new. I am thankful to God who brought me this way. Oh! If the world knew what they are missing out on. All I desire is to be a traditional Catholic mother like the mothers I see on Catholic Finer Femininity blog, emulating the lives of the saints and Our Lady. More I have yet to discover about this ever-new beauty of the church. I heard about interior life for the first time in the TLM and how important it is. The spirituality in the TLM is one founded on the lives of the saints and the traditional teaching of the Church. As the superior general of the FSSP said on his recent visit to the parish in Nigeria "It's not just the Mass but everything that goes with it, the teaching of the faith, following the footsteps of what the Church has been doing for many centuries. It connects us to the past and indeed to the future."

9. EVERYTHING POINTS TO GOD
Emma, Age 14, Tennessee

CLOSE YOUR EYES AND IMAGINE A PLACE where the Eternal and Divine Trinity is adored; where the spotless Lamb Who was offered on the Cross comes down from heaven to live in the hearts of the faithful; where priest and laity join prayers as one voice raised up to the throne of God in the form of hallowed Latin chant; and finally, where sacred silence reigns supreme and Jesus Christ, the Savior of the world, is present in everyone's minds, hearts and souls. This is the Traditional Latin Mass. This Mass has made me truly aware of the Supreme Sacrament, that is the Eucharist, and has inspired in me a spirit of reverence and awe for the Eternal God, living and true. But why does this Mass mean so much to me?

To begin, the silence present at this Holy Sacrifice is vital to the sanctity of the Latin Mass. This silence inspires reverence, awe and humility in the souls of all who are present. This said principle kindles great love and fear for the Eternal and living God. Silence likewise instils peace and knowledge of God's love deep in the hearts of the faithful. Yet another benefit of silence entails how peace and stillness both point to the mystery of the Living God and the awesome reality of His actual presence in the Sanctuary.

Another fact pertaining to the magnitude of the Latin Mass is found in the verity of the direction to which the priest faces. *Ad Orientem*, meaning "to the east," is the Latin term used to communicate the direction the priest faces during Mass. The priest faces east in order to look toward the rising sun. Hence, churches were built with their doors facing west, for the priest, standing in front of the people, would be looking east. Yet, the temporal direction that the priest faces is not the only benefit of *Ad Orientem* Masses. When the priest stands in front of the people, it is as though he is leading them to Christ. When the host is raised, everything points to God. The congregation's eyes; the priest's hands; and finally, the crucifix looking down upon the faithful, pouring out His love and His Blood in a saving tide of redemption. This not only directs everything toward heaven but is also a symbol of the Christian's journey here on earth, and the leading role that the priest possesses in it. Still another proof of the importance of *Ad Orientem* Masses is found in the fact that, since everything points to God as said before, every person present at Mass is aware that God is the supreme Individual being worshipped; they are aware of their weak and sinful nature, and hence they are mindful of the love God has for them by still inviting them to take part in the Lamb's High Feast. Lastly, when the priest and the people are both facing the same way; that is, towards the Crucifix and the tabernacle, all who are present experience a deep sense of humility as they look toward The One who they know is worthy of all their praise. When the priest is facing the people, it as though there is a conversation taking place between the priest and the people–where the priest has his back toward the tabernacle and Crucifix; it as though the latter and the former have been excluded from the sacrifice of praise even though they are the reason Mass is taking place.

One element of the Latin Mass revealed in its title is the sacred Latin language. It can seem odd that there is a Mass that is celebrated in a language that is allegedly "dead," however, this tongue is almost certainly the most important part of this Mass. Latin was spoken by most of the saints; it has been the language of the church for centuries. Even today, our Holy Father, the Pope, writes his encyclicals and many of his letters in Latin. It is a language that has been blessed by God; this is proved by the aforementioned facts and by many other realities and events. Another reason Latin is so important a language to be used at Mass lies in the fact that, since no one speaks this language, there is no argument necessary over what language is going to be spoken at Mass. Everything is spoken in the same sacred language. *Sacrosanctum Concilium*, written during Vatican II, explicitly clarified that the Latin language was to be preserved: "The use of the Latin language is to be preserved in the Latin Rites" (SC 36).

A fourth fact pertaining to the importance of the Latin Mass in my life and in the lives of many others lies in the use of incense. This sacramental plays a crucial part in the Mass, including blessing the altar, priest, and people. Incense infuses the mind with the love of God and lingers in the air as Jesus lingers in our souls. The prayers during the Canon are our connection to God the Father; the reception of the Eucharist is our connection to God the Son; and finally, the use of Holy Incense is our connection to God the Holy Ghost. Incense acts as the Third Person of the Blessed Trinity acts. He infuses the heart and the mind with love and zeal for the Church and the Truth of the Faith. Lastly, incense brings to mind where Jesus would go to temple when he was on earth, and the high priest would bless the Ark of the Covenant and the inner chamber of the temple with the holy spices. Thus, we discover another connection to Jesus at the Latin Mass.

A fifth topic that cannot be left out consists of the Gregorian Chant that is sung at Mass. This chant was blessed by God through the actions of St. Pope Gregory. St. Pope Gregory loved music, and in the fifth century, he created the *Schola Cantorum* in Rome. This singing school was founded to reorganize the liturgy and include chanting during Mass. Aside from the importance of its historical past, Gregorian chant fills the mind with peace and reverence and knowledge of the Sacrifice of Praise. Much of chant contains reference to the psalms and many other parts of the Bible. There are also several chant songs in honor of Mary and the saints. In brief, Gregorian chant is another vital part of the Liturgy.

The last point that I wish to stress is the use of veils by the women who attend the Traditional Latin Mass. Women who wear veils are likened to Mary, the mother of God; it is very difficult to find a painting of Mary in which she is not clothed in a veil. Should not all women try to imitate their Blessed Lady in every way possible? All things respected and honored are covered with a veil. One reference to this fact is found in the book of Exodus, when the Lord calls Moses to build his holy temple and to cover the holy tabernacle:

> And all the men that were wise of heart, to accomplish the work of the tabernacle, made ten curtains of twisted fine linen, and violet, and purple, and scarlet, twice dyed, with varied work and the art of embroidering: The length of one curtain was twenty-eight cubits, and the breadth four: all the curtains were of the same size. And he joined five curtains, one to another, and the other five he coupled one to another. He made also loops of violet in the edge of one curtain on both sides, and in the edge of the other curtain in like manner (Exodus 36:8-10 DR).

And again: "He made also eleven curtains of goat hair to cover the roof of the tabernacle" (Exodus 36:14 DR).

Yet another proof of this holy fact lies in how we respect our faithful departed. Their faces are covered with a veil as a sign of reverence for the body which God created. Finally, before new life begins in this world, babies are hidden inside their mother. This is another verification that life is sacred and must be preserved and respected. Hence, women should be honored to wear a veil at Mass for it shows that she respects herself and her God-given ability to bring new life into the world.

These six topics are a mere fraction of the reasons why the Latin Mass means so much to me and to so many others. This Sacrifice will never cease to amaze me and inspire in me a spirit of awe for God. To hear the chant and to truly feel the Lord inside my soul. To see so many little children kneeling with their families, aware that Something great is taking place even before they know how to talk, "... so that even the littlest children watched and listened with a kind of awe. They were all aware, even those who did not understand all the words, that what he was reading to them was wonderfully stirring, and that it belonged to all of them... (*Aleko's Island*, Edward Fenton 1948)." This passage is perhaps the best way to describe how we all feel at Mass–it is as if we were all little children who do not truly understand what the priest is reading and saying, but we are aware that It truly belongs to us, and It is the most important thing that can happen on earth. We will never entirely understand this Mystery in full: that Jesus, the Son of God, does come down to earth and is present in every single host that the priest gently distributes. This is the way we can all stay as little children as Jesus said:

> Amen I say to you, unless you be converted, and become as little children, you shall not enter into the kingdom of heaven. Whosoever therefore shall humble himself as this little child, he is the greater in the kingdom of heaven (Matthew18:3–4 DR).

Therefore, let us all become like little children and approach the Great Sacrifice with love and awe so that we may enter the kingdom of heaven; there we will finally understand fully the Mystery which takes place and see the Lamb of God face to face. *Agnus Dei, qui tollit peccata mundi, miserere nobis!*

10. SERVING AT THE TRADITIONAL LATIN MASS
Leo, Age 17, Wisconsin

My experience with the TLM began in 2017 when a group of men at my parish decided to start a Latin Mass community. I was about 10 years old. I had been serving at the Novus Ordo for several years, and I liked where I was at the time. I can't remember much of what went on, but I still remember that one night at the dinner table my dad asked my two brothers and myself how we would like the idea of going to and then serving the Latin Mass. Not knowing much about the TLM, I was a little skeptical of the idea, but we were willing, and I am sure my father was grateful for our willingness to learn and go along with it.

Now, the preparations were already in motion, but for the TLM community we had nothing to work with and were starting from the ground up. There was only one man among us who knew how to serve the TLM or even how it worked. Father was also new to the idea, but he thought it would be good to learn the TLM. So, with a bunch of willing boys and their fathers there was a long string of three-hour practices in which we learned how to serve the Latin Mass. Of course, young boys don't have the greatest attention spans, and I was no exception, not to mention the fact that there is only so much you can learn even with hands-on practices.

In Advent of 2017 the day finally came. I am not sure which Sunday it was, but I do know that the Mass was not seamless. Indeed, we were off to a rocky start and had much to learn, but all things considered we did fine for our first time. The string of long practices continued, and we got much feedback from the server coordinator, the man who had trained us, after Mass on what we had done wrong and how we, as a group, could do better next Sunday. This went on for a few more months until we were well established as a community. In my 10-year-old mind I did not like the TLM or much that went along with it. Being stubborn, I did not enjoy having to learn a long, and seemingly overly complicated Mass which had the same result upon completion. The result being that, if properly disposed, you had received Our Lord in the Holy Eucharist, and had fulfilled your Sunday obligation.

My brothers and I were still serving the Novus Ordo once or twice a month and any Holy days we were asked to serve for. As time went on, we began to get a little annoyed with some irreverence to Our Lord that we saw in the Novus Ordo which we did not see in the Latin Mass. We also saw that with the way the two Masses were structured, Our Lord received much more reverence and glorification in the Latin Mass than in the Novus Ordo. For instance, in the Novus Ordo it is a common sight to see Our Lord received in the hand and not on the tongue, resulting in particles of the consecrated host, which is now Our Lord, being dropped all over the place, being trampled on, when every particle deserves all respect, and every possible measure taken so that He receives due reverence. Though what goes on with communion in the hand is a debate for another time, even as a 10-year-old boy I could see the problems with it, and the disrespect to Our Lord was very irritating to me.

Another example of greater reverence shown in the TLM is the way the ablutions are conducted and handling of the sacred vessels. In the Novus Ordo, it is common to see the servers and other lay people handling the sacred vessels such as the Chalice and the Patten as if they were ordinary everyday objects. While with the TLM, that is greatly discouraged since if the vessels have been blessed, and they have been used in the sacrifice of the Mass, they have come in direct contact with Our Lord, and now should not encounter the unconsecrated hands of a lay person. Since priests and deacons have their hands consecrated, they can come into direct contact with the Eucharist and the Sacred Vessels. Now, my point is not to get into a philosophical debate on why things can and can't be done, it is to show what I saw from the perspective of a young boy, and why now as a teenager I have great love and respect for the TLM.

As time went on, we, my brothers and I, started to love the Latin Mass for its reverence and its Gregorian chant, and even the challenge that properly serving it presents. I feel as if there is something to the TLM that is somewhat masculine and attracts men, though I have not figured out exactly what that is yet. At the TLM there are so many young men who want to return every week, and if the occasion arises, they will bring themselves, either with their family or alone, to the TLM.

Back to the story. I was probably eleven at this time, and I wanted to stop serving the Novus Ordo entirely, and only attend the Latin Mass. And then came Holy Week. I am not sure which year it was, either 2018 or 2019, but after serving the Novus Ordo Holy Thursday mass, we were finally able to figure out a way to voice our disgust and discontent with what we were seeing in the Novus Ordo. When we voiced our complaints to Dad, he said that he had been seeing some of the same issues. From that point on until after *Traditionis Custodes* came out, with the exception of the lockdown during Covid, we attended the TLM at our parish every Sunday. Before, and especially after Covid, I grew tremendously in my faith life. I attribute this to the TLM and the wonderful community we had at my parish.

After *Traditionis Custodes* came out we were told that we couldn't have the TLM at our parish anymore. Our community was in an uproar about having to leave our parish if we wished to attend the TLM. By the grace of God, we still have a church near us where we can go to the TLM, the Shrine of Our Lady of Guadalupe in La Crosse WI. There are two parishes worth of people that attend the TLM there every Sunday.

This being said, I still attend a Novus Ordo mass every so often at my old parish. This Novus Ordo is said similarly to the way a Low Mass might be, though it is not in Latin and there are a lot of missing parts. The way that things are done is more reverent than at the average parish, though there are still the lectors and some people receiving standing up. These things I can forgive if it means I can go to mass and receive the Eucharist during the week. I do not think I would be where I am today had we not found the Latin Mass.

Throughout the course of this essay, it has been my aim to avoid making or bringing up abstract arguments either for the TLM or against the Novus Ordo. Instead, I have attempted to deliver what is seen in the Latin Mass through the eyes of a young boy, and how his views on it changed as he grew older. The point of this was to provide a new view on the TLM that perhaps has not been thought about before. I have attempted to provide just the facts and to let you, the reader, make up your mind on the subject. I pray that this essay accurately depicts the beauty of the TLM. To God be the glory!

11. THE GLORIOUS HARMONY AND SANCTITY OF THE TRADITIONAL LATIN MASS
Isabella, Age 17, Tennessee

I HAVEN'T ALWAYS ATTENDED THE TRADITIONAL Latin Mass. For the first 12 years of my life, my family and I attended an irreverent Novus Ordo Mass in a building under a gym that could easily have passed as a Protestant meeting room. After we realized that this must not be the best way to worship God, we found a more reverent parish where they used some Latin and said Mass *ad orientem*. But it wasn't until I was 15 that we found the Traditional Latin Mass. One of my favorite descriptions of it is a "barbed entrance:" like an arrow or a fishhook with a barb; the arrow can enter its target, or the fish can bite the hook, but then the barbs on the arrow and the hook prevent the arrow from coming out of the target and the fish from releasing itself from the hook. Likewise, now that I have had a taste of the TLM, I am stuck fast, and there is no way that I can go back to the Novus Ordo. There's absolutely no way that I can ever go back to the Novus Ordo, now that I have had a taste of the TLM.

When I really sit down and try to figure out why I love the TLM, a thousand reasons come up all at once, but at the heart of it is my love for the Blessed Sacrament. Since the Blessed Sacrament *is* Our Lord—Body, Blood, Soul, and Divinity—and we are commanded to love Him with all our heart, soul, mind, and strength, it hurts me to see Him present in the Novus Ordo simply because the "New Mass" doesn't glorify Him as He deserves. Like a jeweler who has a precious diamond, I can't bear to see the diamond set in a cheap, tarnished setting. I know that the diamond deserves better. In the Traditional Mass, I can tell that Our Lord is set in the ring He deserves.

I know that the TLM glorifies Our Lord the most not only because it is the Mass approved and offered by the Catholic Church for two millennia, but also because this Mass combines Heaven and Earth in the most glorious, harmonious way possible. In the TLM, we use our bodies and earthly resources as they are meant to be used: to glorify God and to manifest our faith. Since God created both human beings and the Earth to glorify Himself, the best way that we can praise and love Him is by using ourselves and our earthly resources for His glory. God could have created human beings as pure spirits, like angels, but He did not. Instead, He created us as physical, incarnational beings. We can see, taste, feel, smell, and hear. The TLM uses all these gifts that God gave to us to praise Him and to direct us towards Him.

In addition to glorifying God through the use of our physical means, the TLM fulfills Our Lord's command to us to become like little children. When we attend the TLM, it is impossible for us not to notice how holy and sacred it is, and our faith in what we *cannot* see is reinforced by the physical manifestation of the things we *can* see. I have heard of a young boy who said that he "felt" God in the Latin Mass. Children who attend the Latin Mass have a "leg up" in their religious education; they learn what is going on by experiencing it—by seeing, tasting, smelling, feeling, and hearing it. While adults and older children understand what is occurring at Mass simply because they have read about it or been taught about it, it does no harm to have their faith reinforced by the physical experience of the Mass; rather, it pleases Our Lord more when we participate physically in the Mass, rather than merely learn about it, because by doing so, we become like little children who understand because they see; like the apostles who merely heard Our Lord say, "follow Me," and obeyed.

Having attended the Novus Ordo Mass for much of my childhood, the relative clarity and physical harmony of the TLM stand out to me in so many different instances of the Mass, from the prayers at the foot of the altar, to the direction of the priest, to the reception of Holy Communion on the tongue, to the Last Gospel. Noticing these ancient, prayerfully developed particularities in the TLM has strengthened not only my faith, but also my love of God. The TLM has led me closer to Heaven than I thought was possible on earth.

The whole orientation of the TLM leads us closer to Heaven. Both priest and people face the same direction. If one were to look at the TLM from above, it would appear that priest and people, as a unified body, were prostrate before the altar in an attitude of supplication and prayer, and it would also be apparent that the main focus of the Mass is on the front of the Church, on the altar and the Tabernacle. This is perfectly appropriate since the altar is essentially where two worlds—heaven and earth—meet. The altar, where Christ becomes present during the Mass, is the mid-point of this meeting of worlds; also appropriate since Christ is the mediator between Heaven and

The Glorious Harmony and Sanctity of the Traditional Latin Mass

earth. Traditionally, churches were built around this reality; altars were fixed to the wall, in fact, so that there was no room at all for anyone to walk between the altar and the Tabernacle, between Heaven and Earth. Additionally, churches were built facing east, in the direction of the Holy Land, where Christ lived while on earth. Thus, by the orientation of the earthly things—priest, people, and church building—the Heavenly truths of the Mass are communicated to us, and our attitude of prostration and supplication to God using our physical bodies brings glory to Him.

Another way in which the TLM draws us closer to God and Heaven is by its music. One of the greatest gifts God has given to us is our voices; without them, we could not communicate. But God also made our voices capable of producing beautiful, melodious sounds when we sing. The Latin Mass makes the best use of this gift of song by directing it toward God in beautiful, traditional music. The beauty and order of the prescribed Gregorian chant reflects the beauty and order of God, just as the Latin language does. Chant is profoundly beautiful and solemn; one only has to hear it to understand that we are in the presence of something holy and sacred. As Catholics, we acknowledge that there is objective Truth, so we understand that some forms of music are suited for the Holy Sacrifice, and some are not. Much of the music of the TLM is written by saints, popes, and holy men and women, and it is written to be beautiful, sacred, and pleasing to God. Many of the most wonderful works of music in the world were written by famous composers for Traditional Masses. When I attend the TLM, I always find that the music seems to direct me towards God, and to reflect His beauty, wisdom, and harmony.

As the name suggests, Latin is the primary language used in the TLM. I love the Latin language; not only is it the language of my Church, but it is also profoundly beautiful, pleasing to the tongue, and well organized. The Latin language is governed by very strict rules; because of these rules, learning Latin is more like a puzzle than a language class. Every noun has its declension, and every verb has its conjugation. Sure, there are some irregularities, but for the most part, Latin is easy to understand because it is made up of regular rules. The strict order of the language reflects the wonderful order of God; I think this is one of the reasons that we have never, as humans, but especially as Catholics, completely let Latin go. Scientific names are all in Latin; many modern languages are derived from it. Even in the modern day, the pope still releases documents in Latin.

When the Mass is said in Latin, it communicates to us how sacred and beautiful the Mass actually is; how different it is from our daily lives and conversation. And because we do not hear Latin every day, it is a new and pleasing sound to our ears. We are told in the Psalms to sing a new song to the Lord; Latin is new to us, and it is beautiful, like a song! Additionally, because Latin is no longer a spoken language in any part of the world, it is a what we call a "dead language." This means that the meaning of Latin words will not change, whereas some vernacular words do change due to the wide usage they receive in everyday life. For instance, the meaning of the English word "awful" has completely changed over the years; once, the word literally meant, "full of awe," suggesting something magnificent and great. However, the word "awful" has evolved to describe something terrible or frightening. Because the Latin language is no longer in use as a spoken language, we can be sure that it will be preserved in its purity and unchanged in its meaning. For all of these reasons and because it was the language of the ancient Roman empire, Latin is the language of the Catholic Church. Even Vatican II documents (written in Latin) speak of the importance of the Latin language. When the Mass is said in Latin, we are hearing and speaking the beautiful language of our fathers in Faith.

Though the TLM is *said* in Latin, much of the Mass is actually *heard* only by God, the priest, and the altar boys. The silence during so many parts of the Mass is so beautiful and helpful to our faith. When the priest says the Mass silently, we are aware that He is truly speaking to God. This is not some theatrical production where we, as spectators, are most important and are meant to hear everything that is said. Rather, we are only very minor characters in this tremendous drama of Christ's sacrifice; the monumental events taking place here are all about God; thus, the priest's primary focus is upon Him, not us.

In the Novus Ordo Mass, where silence is wanting, I find that the clamorous noise of the human voice detracts from the sense of the sacred. The noise diminishes my awareness that the moment of consecration is the holiest in all the world. I can think of nothing more profound, more sacred, more holy, than that single moment where the priest, in holy awe, whispers the words of consecration. After all, Christ did not herald His coming into this world with the voices of trumpets; instead, He chose to be born in a humble stable where only the Holy Family and the Shepherds were present. On Mount Sinai, too, God chose to become present to Moses not in the earthquake, wind, or fire, but in the still, small voice. When the priest whispers in a similar small voice, it also distinguishes the nobility of his priestly vocation. We, the laypeople, are not worthy or prepared to hear the words of consecration, since we have not received the Sacrament of Holy Orders. I think that when the priest says Mass aloud to the people, not only does the Mass become more about the congregation, but it also takes away from our sense of the sacred and our appreciation of the priesthood.

When I began to understand more fully the dignity of the Holy Sacrifice, I noticed that the more "separate," in a sense, that the clergy and laity become, the greater our joyful humility becomes. When we, as laypeople, attempt to "participate" in the liturgy by making ourselves equal with the priest, we are not only disrespecting God Himself and the clergy, but also ourselves by not understanding the reverence which we are obliged to pay to God. If laypeople and clergy could do the same jobs, why would God have instituted the priesthood in the first place?

Another priceless aspect of the Latin Mass is the prayers at the foot of the altar. The Latin Mass is begun at the foot of the altar; the priest and the altar servers stand before God and, before ascending to offer the Holy Sacrifice, they ask God to prepare them and purify them of their sins. What better way to enter into the glory of the Holy Mass! Just as we certainly wouldn't arrive at a party without first having prepared our bodies, so we cannot begin the Holy Mass without first preparing our souls. While private prayers before Mass are excellent and necessary, these public prayers of preparation draw us into the Mass and force us to get our souls in order and ready for the Holy Sacrifice.

I absolutely love the distinction which the Latin Mass makes between men and women, emphasizing the dignity of both sexes which God created. The role of altar servers and priests, only performed by males in the Tridentine rite, are essential to the Latin Mass. The necessity of priests is self-evident. Servers pray the responses at the foot of the altar, move the missal from one side of the altar to the other, help the priest prepare the altar and incense, incense the faithful at the offertory, hold the priest's chasuble at the Consecration, bear the Communion-plates as the Eucharist is distributed, and perform so many other important functions at the Mass. Altar boys and priests perform the "work" at the Mass: they prepare the way for the Lord and serve Him actively.

In contrast, the women at the Latin Mass sit quietly in the Sanctuary, veiled and dignified. Some women praise God through raising their beautiful, feminine voices to Him in small church choirs. Others perform the duty of mothers: to watch over their children and to teach them what is occurring at this Holy Mass. Many others simply sit in the congregation and participate in the Holy Mass in the veiled sanctuaries of their hearts. God gave men strong bodies suited to work; women's bodies, while not as strong, are created to accomplish beautiful mysteries on the *inside*. As Venerable Archbishop Fulton Sheen said, it is the job of the woman to *receive* what is being prepared—to simply sit and adore Our Lord through the beauty of themselves and in the quiet peace of their souls. There is a beauty about the quiet, humble, fragility of women that God uses to His purpose in the Latin Mass. A wise priest once told me that he greatly appreciated when women wore veils, because veiling is a way to respect that which bears life. It is for this reason that the Tabernacle is veiled, or has a veil inside, and the Sacred Vessels are veiled when they enter the Sanctuary. There is nothing so touching as the sight of a lovely young woman, veiled and kneeling in prayer. Likewise, there is nothing so inspiring as a devout altar boy performing his important duties in the Mass with care and purpose. Both roles inspire respect in observers. By emphasizing the difference in men and women, the Latin Mass emphasizes the dignity of each in a way that is not achieved by giving the same roles to both.

The greatest aspect of all in the Latin Mass is the manner of receiving Holy Communion. In the TLM, communicants kneel at the altar rail, as though they are at a very sacred table. They watch as Jesus approaches, carried by the Priest and escorted by altar boys with Communion-plates. Our Lord is placed upon the tongue of those whom He has desired to visit. The communicants themselves say nothing, do nothing. Because of this, they are completely subject to God. They receive Him directly into their mouths, like helpless baby birds receive life-giving food from their tender mothers. (One of the saints' favorite titles for Our Lord is *Pie Pellicane*, or "loving pelican," because pelicans are known to feed their young with their own blood if food is scarce.) In the Latin Mass, laypeople do not touch the Holy Eucharist; we are aware that it is only for priests, those whose hands have been consecrated with holy oils and whose souls have been endowed with special graces, to touch Our Lord Himself. Kneeling there at the altar rail, preparing to receive Our Lord, I have realized that I don't really want to touch Him, and I don't want to speak. I want to appear full of awe and adoration before Him, my King and my God. I want to show Him with my physical body that I really am totally His, and that I abandon myself to Him like a child in the arms of his loving Father.

In the TLM, Our Lord does *more* than just come into our souls, even though this is the greatest privilege we could ever imagine: He also blesses us with the Sign of the Cross and gives us the graces to come with Him to everlasting life in heaven. And He gives us this blessing in Latin, through the words of the priest: "*Corpus Domini Nostri, Iesu Christi, custodiat animam tuam in vitam aeternam*," "May the Body of Our Lord, Jesus Christ, safeguard your soul unto eternal life." As the priest blesses us with the Most Holy Eucharist, and then administers the Host to us, the altar boys guard the Host with the Communion-plates, lest even a crumb of Our Lord fall to the floor. How beautiful this Sacrament is, and how wonderfully it communicates to little children the love and concern which Our Blessed Lord has for us, and which we should have for Him!

After the reception of Holy Communion, the priest at the Latin Mass performs the ablutions of the sacred vessels, and the Mass draws to a close. However, instead of merely ending after the final prayers, the Latin Mass also provides us with a last, beautiful passage of Sacred Scripture to "send us off" and to remind us of the wonder and glory of the Lord whom we have just received. This passage is known as the Last Gospel and is the beginning of the Gospel of St. John. Reading the words of the Last Gospel and knowing that St. John was Jesus' beloved disciple, I cannot help but feel that St. John, in an ecstasy of joy and love, simply poured forth the words which I hear after the Latin Mass straight from His heart. And this is exactly the attitude which we should have after receiving Our Lord: pure, profound joy and love for Him Who gave Himself to us. The Last Gospel is the best, most perfect "wrap-up" for the Holy Mass. Its words are full of beauty and remind us how we must live if we hope to become true sons of God.

I have written about many of the beauties, harmonies, and perfections of the Latin Mass. Yet I think there is something more; something which makes the Latin Mass seem so very holy, grand, sublime, and perfect; something above our human reason. I think it is just that this Mass is so very pleasing to God. When we pray the Latin Mass, we cannot help but come closer to Him. We are praying the greatest prayer on earth, and not just on earth, but in Heaven, too! We are praying the same Mass that the apostles and saints have prayed, and we are really present at Christ's Sacrifice of Himself. This Mass has not been tampered with, has not been changed, has not been altered; in fact, this Mass was created by the Lord Himself, working through His Church.

I love to think of the happiness we cause Our Lord to feel when we search out the Latin Mass—when we spend most of our Sundays in the car, get up in the wee hours of the morning, even attend Mass in basements or meeting halls because the TLM is not welcome in so many church buildings—simply because we know how much He is glorified in the Tridentine Mass. I pray that so many of the shepherds of the Church who do not understand the TLM will open their hearts to its glory, its beauty, and its perfection. I pray that they will champion the Sacred Tradition of the Lord Whom they serve.

12. "HE'S NOT A TAME LION"
Annabella, Age 14, New Jersey

I HAVE GONE TO THE TLM SINCE THE FIRST Sunday my mom went to church after my birth. As a kid, I thought the usual kid thing that the TLM was boring, and the Novus Ordo mass was more fun. But then I learned the timeless history, and the language. There are many aspects to love about the Traditional Latin mass. It's been around for over 1,900 years, the music is beautiful, and yes, it's in a different language but that's part of the fun.

I truly fell in love with the TLM when I started using a Missal. I realized just how profound and poetic each hymn is. Also, having the exact words of the Mass allowed me to memorize nearly the entire common of the Mass, and this past Easter I shocked my parents by memorizing the *Vidi Aquam*.

Gregorian chant is one of my favorite parts of the TLM, and the fact that it's in Latin is what makes it so good. Imagine the Credo sung with Gregorian chant, but in English. It doesn't have the same majestic power as the Latin does.

The Nicene Creed was one of the first things that fascinated me. At least to the history geek that I became, a bunch of bishops coming together against Arius to make a list of Catholic dogmas was exciting. And the sound of the Creed sung in Latin has always come across as inspiring, especially the Incarnatus.

When I walk into the church building, I have a feeling that there is something great dwelling in there. The surrounding music wafts me in a deep feeling of love and spirituality. The entire church, except for the choir and the celebrant and the occasional baby, is quiet and reverent. Because of how the mass is celebrated, I don't have to be very involved. The servers are there to pray the mass, and I can focus on my faith and personal prayers. I always drift out of worldly reality into the reality of the faith.

The TLM has a greater feeling of reverence and necessity. It conveys the truth that God is truly the High King and must be worshiped accordingly. Fridays are mandatory days of abstinence, Holy days of obligation aren't moved to the following Sunday for convenience, there is a strict dress code.

I even enjoy the dress code for the TLM. When I was very little, I read something in a children's book about how to dress for the mass. It talked about how you would dress when visiting a king, and how you shouldn't greet the king wearing ripped jeans and a T-shirt. Sometimes children's books are smarter than the adult ones.

The TLM helps you along by encouraging you to take up your cross and carry it with a loving faith. Not to say that the TLM makes it *impossible* to throw away the cross, but it can help you to bear it. It doesn't enforce the rules of the faith in a tyrannical way. The true reason that we fast and pray is out of love and charity, and nothing else. It can be hard with all these rules to do it purely out of love. But again, it's all part of the test.

Why? Because God is the greatest of all, and He requires this of us. In the words of C. S. Lewis, "he is not a tame lion." God doesn't want for our lives as a Catholic to be flexible, because then it's not a thorough test. He allows for Catholicism to be a cross to be sure that we truly love him. If one attempts to make the Catholic life easier than the necessary cross is tossed aside, and we fail the test.

We as Catholics know for sure that Jesus Christ supports the way of worship in the Latin mass because He invented it Himself. He himself showed the Apostles exactly how to do the important things, mainly the consecration. The language doesn't matter, but it instills the fact that the TLM has hardly changed since the Last Supper 2,000 years ago.

The Traditional Latin Mass gives you that feeling of God being great from the moment you genuflect before entering the church, all the way to when you genuflect before exiting. This Fear of the Lord isn't just a little extra something, it's a necessity. It's necessary to fear the Lord because if we don't, we'll turn against Him. Just like how kids are more likely to love their parents if they have discipline, we are more likely to love God if we fear and honor him. Love is key, but not the feeling of love — the *act* of love. The feeling of love is nothing but a fleeting moment of preference. True, deep love is the willingness to give everything to someone. To be charitable, faithful, and hopeful in someone.

In conclusion, what makes the TLM different is the rigorous and humble mindset. The enforcement of loving diligence. The Latin Mass shows the Kingship of the Lord through reverence, beautiful music and the grandeur of the churches. I love it to the bottom of my soul and will continue to love it to my dying day.

13. MAY THE LATIN MASS LIVE FOREVER
Sean, Age 16, Louisiana

I WAS NOT BORN INTO THE TRADITIONAL LITurgy like some people, but my family started going when I was very young. My parents did not know about the TLM at all until my mom's friend told her about it and said we should go. Then a little while later my family started going when I was around three or four years old. We did not go every week. At first, we would only go once or twice a month, driving roughly 45 minutes to get there. As a little kid I really did not want to go. I had to wake up early and I would be bored during the long drive. So, most times when my mom said that we were going to the Latin Mass I would be kind of upset. But now I wonder how I ever could have disliked the Latin Mass. I guess I did not understand the beauty of it yet, didn't understand how the amount of reverence mattered, but I do now.

I don't remember much from when I was little, however when I was 10 years old, I desperately wanted to become an altar server, mainly because my brother served and because it looked interesting and different than what I normally did during Mass. I had a deep yearning that I could not explain. I was told I had to wait until I was 11 years old to be an altar server, which I did not like at the time. I waited for a whole year and waiting that whole year only made me want to serve even more and to be closer to God, as close as I could. So, on the Sunday when I had turned 11 I was finally allowed to serve, and it was such a wonderful day! It has been embedded in my memory ever since, and I hope I never forget the joy that I felt when I was finally allowed to serve the TLM.

The beauty of the Mass and the overall reverence at the TLM brings me such joy. The TLM used to seem so strange to me. I could not understand the language, it lasted longer, and it went slower than the Novus Ordo. The TLM seemed slower at first, because I did not understand it, I was bored, and I wasn't following along as well as I should have but I eventually did. I felt that there was more reverence at a TLM, especially once I really paid attention and learned what reverence was. Once I started serving and learning more about the Mass, I understood why reverence was important. It is important because God is infinitely good, He gave His only son Jesus Christ to die for us so that we may go to Heaven and be with Him, and that demands the greatest level of devotion during Mass, which is when Calvary, at the moment Christ was crucified, is on the altar. Once I learned this, I saw the Mass in a completely different light; it was almost as if I was experiencing Mass for the first time all over again.

Whenever I am at Mass and I hear the choir singing in Latin, I feel as though I am very close to Heaven. I feel as though I am in a special place that is on earth but not of earth at the same time. The smell of incense makes my heart feel light and brings back memories of masses from years ago. When I serve, I feel happy at the end of the day because I was so close to our Lord during the sacrifice of the mass, and I feel satisfied that I did something well that day. I do not know what exactly made me fall in love with the Latin Mass, it was probably a combination of many different things, like the language, once I started to understand it, the level of reverence that was shown even when Mass was not being said.

I hope that I will always have access to a Latin Mass that is somewhat close to me, and even if I do not, the Latin Mass will always be close to my heart. It changed how I saw my faith, the people there were a good influence on me and helped me to mature and learn how to be a better person. I could go to any Latin Mass in the world and feel at home and know what is going on even if the people spoke a different language.

I have such good memories of the Latin Mass that I cannot imagine staying away from it for a very long time. There are times when I am not always able to go to a Latin Mass, like when I am on vacation or visiting family and at those times, I do have to go to a Novus Ordo Mass. I will at times feel almost home sick and out of place because I am not used to going to a Novus Ordo anymore. But the Novus Ordo is still a Mass and I attend it with the same reverence as I would if it were in Latin because it is still our Lord on that altar. Even if everyone else is not reverent I still am because that is something that I have learned from the Latin Mass. We must be reverent no matter what happens because God deserves all of our reverence.

I hope the Latin Mass will stay alive forever because it has changed my life, and it has changed so many other lives for the better. Some people's faith is rekindled when they go to a Latin Mass. Others find it hard when they go for the first time but after a while, they too fall in love with it and wish to never be kept from going. I have a friend who was going to his local church and did not like how the people behaved and dressed at his church, but he heard of my church, and he decided to see what a Latin Mass was like. He told me that it astonished him and that it was such a beautiful Mass that he kept coming back. He eventually started serving with me and has become a great altar server and friend. I hope that more people like him will continue to find peace and satisfaction when they go to a Latin Mass, and I hope that those who already go to the Latin Mass will stay because they love it as much as I do and that they will help others to discover this beautiful liturgy.

14. FIRST AND LASTING IMPRESSIONS OF THE TRADITIONAL LATIN MASS
Daniella, Age 14, Perth, Australia

MY FIRST REACTION TO THE TRADITIONAL Latin Mass was, *"It's so long! And so boring!"* The congregation at the Latin Mass barely participate in the Mass. We mostly just sit, stand, and kneel as required. So why is it so incredibly captivating to an astonishing amount of people?

The average time of a normal weekday Mass in a Novus Ordo church is around half an hour, with a Sunday Mass being about an hour. In the Latin Mass? Weekday Masses can take up to an hour, while Sunday Masses can be more than an hour. In the TLM the priest faces *ad orientem* and away from the congregation. Some people may find this uncomfortable and not spiritual. Therefore, Vatican II called for changes in the Mass which were implemented in 1969. It was so people could understand the Mass better and more actively participate. So why are people still hanging on to the old way of praise and worship?

My mother started to home school me around 2018. She used to take me to St Anne's church to learn Latin. This was my first time going to a church that had Latin Mass. Two churches in Western Australia say Latin Mass. One is around half an hour's drive from my house and the other is farther away. I had never been to the Latin Mass before, so everything was new to me. The priest faced away from me, we never participated, and I had to wear a veil. At first, I dreaded going for these long Masses. Then I joined the Legion of Mary about three years later. It was a group where a couple of other children my age and I would go and sit in the hall and pray the rosary and have catechism lessons on a Thursday evening. This was where I really started to get hooked on the Latin Mass.

My dad was in hospital at the time for cancer and my mom, after dropping me off at the Legion of Mary, would go to visit him. This meant I was forced to stay at church and attend Mass after the Legion of Mary. I would sit with my friends during mass and follow along in the little Latin-English mass booklets they had there. I slowly started to like going, and when my dad came out of hospital and I didn't have to go for Mass anymore, I asked my mom to stay for Mass. I had friends there and they all went there for Sunday Mass. At this point, I was still going to my local Novus Ordo church for Sunday Mass, where I was altar serving. I told my friends at Latin Mass that I, a girl, was altar serving at Novus Ordo, and they didn't believe me, as only boys were permitted to alter serve at Latin Mass. I remember one of the boys making a joke about how boy altar servers are called servers, so girl altar servers must be called serviettes!

Going to the Latin Mass was becoming regular for me now, as I went every Thursday. My friends somehow convinced me to go on Sundays too, so my family became regulars at St Anne's. I loved, and still do love, the smell of incense. It tickles my nose, and the smell always thrills me. When I went to the Novus Ordo, they would only use incense for special occasions, so whenever I smell it, I always feel like something special is going to happen. In the Latin Mass, they use incense for all Masses, even weekday Masses. That is one of my favourite things about the Latin Mass. It always feels like something special is going to happen, and the smoke feels like something magical or mysterious is about to take place. In my opinion, this symbolises that every Mass offered is a special mass and should be revered as such.

Another thing I would like to add is that the Latin Mass is full of young people. When I go to a Novus Ordo Mass, most of the congregation is made up of older people. At the TLM everywhere you look there are young people. Young couples, teenagers, babies, toddlers, and everything in between. There are also large families, young families who are just starting, and of course, there are elderly people too. They certainly add life to the liturgy, as you can hear at least one baby throughout the duration of the mass!

I think people love the Latin Mass because of how touching and natural it is. It is free and follows the old rite. I think this in a sense is already what draws people to it. Everything in the Latin Mass is different from the Novus Ordo Masses. From the way the priest says it, to the congregation and the music. The music is old-style music, something you don't hear nowadays. There is something even about the people who go there. They are pious and devoted to not only the Latin Mass but to God and Jesus. They dress their very best every Sunday, as you should for the Lord. The women wear dresses, and the men wear suits.

In our tiny church, we have around 600 people who come for Sunday Mass. This is too much for the building to hold, so a common sight you will see if you pass our church is people standing outside and a speaker to project sound. We also have a cafe at our church, in the hall. We serve food that has been donated, and we accept donations for it. It is to raise money for the upkeep of the church. The people who work there are all volunteers. I sometimes help too.

So, my reaction to the Latin Mass after going through all this? It is very deep and touching. It touches people in ways some wouldn't expect. My parents are godparents to two new converts and last year we had a confirmation and holy communion ceremony with around 60 children who received the sacraments. There are always baptisms going on and it is a very active church and community of which I am very happy to be a part of. I now play the pipe organ there for Sunday mass. I have made some very good friends, and I hope everyone else will have the same amazing experience as me.

15. THE SERENITY OF THE TRADITIONAL LATIN MASS
John, Age 18, Massachusetts

"What does the traditional Latin Mass mean to me?" When I first heard this question, I figured that the only thing I could come up with was that the Latin Mass was "different" from your regular Novus Ordo Mass. However, when I thought about this question more and more, I was surprised to figure out how important the Latin Mass is to me and how big of a role it played throughout my life.

As Catholics, we must learn about our faith and the truths that the Church teaches, for it is the only way we truly know God and believe in Him wholeheartedly. This is especially true when it comes to learning about the Holy Sacrifice of the Mass, which should be the center of every Catholic's life. Within my life, I sincerely believe that the beauty and devotion of the Traditional Latin Mass has done wonders building who I am as a person, and I want to share that with you so that you might also attend and experience the Latin Mass at least once.

I was born and raised a Catholic by very devout and good parents. To give me a good Catholic upbringing, my parents sent me to a Catholic school near my home. My family and I went to a Novus Ordo Mass every Sunday, followed by Sunday school classes. Although my parents tried their hardest to instill within me a belief in God and His Church, it was difficult for me to understand it. There was barely any emphasis on the reality that Christ is within the Eucharist, that He is offering Himself to His Father for our sins. I felt as though I was just going through the motions, I felt no connection to the faith.

But a turning point in my life occurred when some friends of my parents suggested they send me and my siblings to a Catholic school half an hour away. Hearing that the teachers, mostly nuns and monks, were excellent, and the school had daily mass, my parents decided to send me and my siblings there. However, my parents did not know that the mass they celebrated every day happened to be the Traditional Latin Mass.

At first, I was very against the idea of going to a new school, for it meant that I had to leave my friends behind, to wake up an hour earlier so that I could get to school on time (although I never did get to school on time anyways). However, as I got to know the people there more and how kind they were, I started to like the school more and more. But the most important thing I saw was how happy they were, even when they had to live in the same area for the rest of their lives, and their routine was almost the same every day, they had this energy around them that made them feel as though they were content in life, that this was all they needed to be happy.

As time passed, I soon realized their joy stemmed from their Catholic faith, and how much it meant to them. But most importantly, they have a special devotion to the Mass, with it being the center of everything they do. Because of this revelation, I slowly became more interested in my faith and the history of the Church. This increased curiosity eventually led me to try and understand more about the Mass, especially the Latin Mass, which was celebrated at my school. As I studied and attended the Mass more, I began to see how intricate it was and appreciated how this form of worship has been perfected for thousands of years solely to give God the best form of reverence that can be offered. When I read the prayers said throughout the Mass, I am always in awe of how beautiful each prayer is and how it relates to God and our salvation.

When it comes to my spiritual life, the Traditional Latin Mass has transformed how I understand my faith and what is going on in the Sacrifice of the Mass. It has made me grow to love God more and further acknowledge the sacrifice He made for us, which is suffering and dying on the cross. Every time I attend the Latin Mass, I can't help but feel that there is something special happening on the altar, that someone is waiting within that Tabernacle for me. The Latin Mass, which emphasizes Christ's sacrifice for us to His Father, has helped me believe that Christ's body and blood are truly present within that tiny piece of bread and that He is waiting there for me. As I keep attending the Traditional Latin Mass, I always feel a type of serenity that I don't get anywhere else, that everything that is happening in my life is not worth the time I stay in the Church and genuinely offer myself to God in the mass.

The Traditional Mass has also encouraged me to think about and ponder questions that I would have not given much thought to before such as "Is God truly in that small tabernacle?" and "What is my worth?" It has made me think that God is always there with me, helping me answer these questions, even if they might be answered in a way I was not expecting. The Latin Mass has made me see that no matter how imperfect I am, no matter how many times I fall into sin, Christ is always waiting there in that tabernacle for me, to give me the chance to lay down everything to Him. The comforting thought that God is always in the Tabernacle waiting for me to talk to Him always provides me the strength to become the best version of myself. Whenever I feel overwhelmed by something, or there is something big I need to decide upon, when I see Christ's body and blood in the center of the Church, I can't help but forget everything at that moment, offering everything up to God.

Overall, the Traditional Latin Mass is the most beautiful and serene form of worship I can offer to God. It elevates the value of the Eucharist to me and shows me what the Mass is truly about, which is offering, together with the priest, a perfect sacrifice to God, who has given us everything we have. As someone who is now discerning the priesthood so that I can celebrate the Holy Sacrifice of the Mass, I believe that the Traditional Latin Mass has transformed me and my relationship with the Church. I can't imagine what kind of person I would be if I was not exposed to it. It has encouraged me to learn more about my faith, to understand why Catholicism is the one true faith, and why it is so important to be open to change, no matter where it comes from.

16. "THE LATIN MASS BRINGS PEACE TO MY HEART"
Colette, Age 14, Wisconsin

THE TRADITIONAL LATIN MASS IS A BEAUTIFUL sacrifice that I am privileged to go to.

From as far back as I can remember, at the young age of nine or ten, I always attended a Novus Ordo Mass on Sunday. This Mass was great, and the priests were awesome, but, at the time, I wasn't old enough to care much about the Mass. The Mass we went to was right in town and was at nine in the morning. I remember always feeling tired and not ever wanting to go to Mass; I just wanted to sleep in. I would always fall asleep or just play around. I didn't take the Mass seriously.

Around the age of 10 or 11 a consistent Latin Mass came to a nearby town. This town was only twenty minutes away, so my family decided to go. It was a change. Before, the only Latin Masses we would attend were High Masses on feast days and Holy Days of Obligation. Not many of us knew Latin, but we would learn it in school. The priests were nice and welcoming.

Until about a year ago I did not seriously enjoy going to Mass. I thought of it as a burden. I would do everything I could to get out of going to a Mass. Almost every sermon I would fall asleep before we were even halfway through it, and my mind getting distracted constantly. In short, I was not taking my spiritual life seriously. I was looking forward not to Mass, but to talking to cousins and friends afterwards.

Last year rolled around and I was signed up to go to a girls' group an hour away with my sister. This group had about seven or eight girls that I had never met. Before I entered this group, I was very introverted. Being with only new people made me open myself up. This group helped me start to care about my spiritual life. We talked about prayer, saints, and things related to God. At this point in my life, I started to mature and care about what other people were saying. Everything we talked about in the meetings I stored deep in my heart and mind. I realized that I was not very devout or close to the Lord. I realized I needed to pray. Prayer no longer seemed a duty or chore. I wanted to pray. Not just memorized prayers or ones that were written by others. I wanted to pray from the heart.

After strengthening my relationship with God, I realized that I now not only enjoy Mass, but also look forward to it. My brother helps at church and arranges server practices. After these there is a Mass. After going to a few I got to watch what the priest exactly does. I felt more attracted to the Latin Mass. I also got to watch what the servers should and should not do.

I never really liked following along in my missal; I always found it boring and almost useless. I never read the epistle, gospel, or anything that was for that day's Mass. I didn't feel the need to as I thought all that was important was just going to be repeated by the priest in English later. After a year or so of going to Latin Mass, I now love to watch the priest offer up the Great Sacrifice and watch the servers as they go about serving Mass. I can say a lot of the servers' responses.

The Traditional Latin Mass is a beautiful thing. You get to be in the presence of God and feel it. You get to participate in the Mass by way of serving, singing, or just being there and witnessing it. The Latin Mass and the people who attend have made me see how much I needed to change to get closer to God. I needed to be led; rather, I needed to let God lead me. Allowing God to be a bigger part of my life has really opened my eyes to the joys of this world. Before I really, truly attended the Mass, both mentally and physically, I could not control my anger. Now, through prayer, I can push the anger farther back in my solutions list. I am working on totally kicking it off. The Latin Mass brings a peace to my heart, mind, and soul. It makes me feel comforted and loved; it makes me calm. Being able to have this wonderful sacrifice offered every single Sunday in my community has certainly impacted me for the better.

17. AMAZEMENT AT THE SACRIFICE OF JESUS
Zoe, Age 13, Texas

THE TRADITIONAL LATIN MASS EMBRACES THE beauty and reverence that has been part of Catholic worship for thousands of years. It helps us all unite our hearts to Christ on the cross. For me, it is very humbling. Christ bore his cross without complaint, so should we not do likewise? We relive the Passion of our Lord each time we go to the Mass to pray with the priest as he offers it. The Traditional Latin Mass makes me want to become more holy, more devout, and servant-like as I fulfill my duties in my state of life. We should, even when not actively participating in the Mass, make prayers and offerings to our Lord. Our Lord laid down his life for men, so that we all may be saved.

The incense at the Latin Mass creates such a beautiful picture in my mind of these clouds of burning spice being brought to our Lord on high, surrounded by the Saints and Angels of the past with the smoke resembling our prayers, fervently brought to him.

The music and chant of the Latin Mass helps me obtain the right mindset to worship God. Latin is a beautiful, ancient liturgical language, something we do not speak every day. This makes our worship even more special. The music is reverent; it is not meant to be a concert, but it is meant to inspire awe as we unite our prayers with the priest at the altar.

This past year, during the Good Friday Mass, I experienced feelings that made me even more amazed with what Jesus did for me, a poor sinner. During this somber Mass, my heart felt like it was burning, emitting a radiating heat that went all through my body. The church was not warm, and the heat that I felt came from a source within and not like the usual external warmth. This made me embrace the whole tragedy of our Lord's death. When Easter dawned, I felt renewed and experienced a joy that was incomparable to any event. This Easter and Lent was certainly the most moving I have ever felt. It was also my first time worshipping at this sacred time in the year at the Traditional Latin Mass.

The Traditional Liturgy is also so prayerful. For me, since I am learning Latin, it makes everything that I have learned come to life and fruition. The Sacred Liturgy and Mass is what I live for and am willing to die for.

Being at the Traditional Latin Mass helps me keep a proper perspective in my life. What are my goals? What should be my goals? Prayer should be at the center of my day, not temporal deeds or checklists. What are my priorities? What should be my priorities? Assisting at Mass as often as I can, should be my priority, and also living out my vocation as a Catholic and sharing the truth of this beautiful worship.

Our Lord, during his life, showcased the virtues of humility, love, and compassion, with the deepest understanding. This displays the honor due to His name, as He is truly worthy of our exaltation. He cared for the poor and lowly, stooping below His due glory, demonstrating humility. Jesus spoke to all, not favoring the rich or mighty, but giving the same opportunities for salvation to all peoples who believe in Him, showing equality. Furthermore, He went above and beyond, dying for our sins on the cross, signifying His great love for all. If I wrote a paper on each and every triumph of Our Lord, the pages would go on until the end of time. When I think about this, it makes me want to worship him all the more and better when I go to Mass.

"Love is patient and kind; love is not jealous or boastful; it is not arrogant or rude. Love does not insist on its own way; it is not irritable or resentful; it does not rejoice at wrong but rejoices in the right. Love bears all things, believes all things, hopes all things, endures all things. Love never ends; as for prophecies, they will pass away; as for tongues, they will cease; as for knowledge, it will pass away. For our knowledge is imperfect and our prophecy is imperfect; but when the perfect comes, the imperfect will pass away... So faith, hope, love abide, these three; but the greatest of these is love" (1 Cor. 13:4-10, 13 RSV). These are some of my favorite verses because I understand that they represent what we believe and pray for when we worship at the Mass. We must live out our Catholic vocation and display Christian charity to everyone we see. We must have the mindset that we may not receive love in return. Jesus instructed us to love our enemies, and to pray for those who persecute us. Assisting at the Traditional Latin Mass, with its beauty, reverence, and power, makes even greater known to us these important words of love. This makes clear to us that we must follow our Lord's words in every matter out of love for him and His Church.

Writing this essay has even helped me realize how important the Traditional Latin Mass is to me, and how much I love praying in this reverent, wonderful way.

Long live Christ the King and his Church! Christus vincit, Christus regnat, Christus imperat!

18. A BEAUTIFUL HARMONY OF PRAISE TO THE LORD
Elianna, Age 13, Michigan

I FIRST WENT TO A LATIN MASS BECAUSE MY brothers were learning to serve it so they could help to introduce the Latin Mass at our parish. I had no wish to go but went along with them to the Masses. At first, I was confused as to what was going on and frustrated at being unable to participate. Yet when it was over, I still went away thinking that it was beautiful and wanted to learn more about it. My parents found books on the Latin Mass that our family could read. Parts of the liturgy that had seemed unimportant to me suddenly had deep meaning behind them. As we began to go more and more to the Latin Mass and it was finally brought to our parish, I was drawn especially to three things: the time for prayer and contemplation throughout, the beauty that the music and language brought to the liturgy, and the unique parts of the liturgy for every special feast.

The more often we went to the Latin Mass the more I was able to participate. Slowly I learned to follow along and recite the correct words. Yet in the times I was unable to, I spent in prayer or just thinking about the mass so I could understand what was happening. Our priest often advises people, before the mass even begins, to just be there and pray and contemplate. He also says to not follow along, but to turn your thoughts to God and the sacrifice taking place. Because of his explanation, I now understand that I was participating by simply being present and turning my thoughts to God and the mass. I didn't have to worry about saying the right things at the right times, I could simply just be present, thinking and praying. I could think about my worries, what I was struggling with, or even just what I hoped to happen, and throughout the Mass I could place them all before Jesus. Something that helps me while contemplating and praying is the music that the choir chants.

The beauty of the music and the language the prayers are spoken in add a whole new loveliness and mystical element to the mass. I always feel closer to God as I listen to the chanting. Each voice in the choir is unique and is giving thanks to God in their own way. Joined together, they create a beautiful harmony of praise to the Lord.

I can be there and merely focus on listening or I can let the music inspire my prayers and thoughts, leading me to greater virtue. Often at Easter and Christmas our choir brings trumpets, violins, and other instruments to lend more beauty to the Mass. They follow specially composed music for the Latin Mass to make it even more beautiful. At All Soul's they sing a Requiem Mass. The music for this is angelic and hopeful at the same time. The different music that they have throughout the year praises God and honors Mary and the Saints. The tone of the music pulls you in to understand the true depth more fully behind every unique part of the Mass.

There are many feasts throughout the liturgical year. Some that I have been to are Candlemas, the Assumption, Pentecost, and the Feast of Corpus Christi. For each one there is a part of the liturgy that is unique to that feast. At Candlemas there is a blessing of candles and a procession in the dark before mass even begins. There are special prayers and litanies recited for the Assumption, Pentecost, and the Feast of Corpus Christi. These masses are sometimes followed by benediction or processions around the church grounds and through the city. One of my favorite parts about Advent are the Rorate Caeli masses. These masses are to honor the Blessed Virgin and take place before dawn on Saturdays in Advent. Even though most of my family does not prefer early mornings it has still become a family tradition to go to them every year. Rorate Caeli masses begin in the dark with only candles illuminating the church. Besides the many candles dimly lighting the sanctuary, each person holds their own candle flickering against the darkness. When the mass is over, dawn has broken and the sun's rays have pierced the stained-glass windows, filling the church with early morning light.

The few first times I went to the Latin Mass I went hesitantly and because I had to. Yet after only a couple months I came to appreciate it a lot more. I was drawn to it because of all these things, but there is so much more that you learn every time you go to the Latin Mass. Many different people can appreciate it for many different reasons, but for me it was the contemplation and prayer throughout the mass, the beautiful music, and the deep meanings behind each part of the liturgy. All of these things draw me to the mass, but also bring me closer to God.

19. "MY SOUL WAS DYING OF STARVATION BEFORE"
Andrea, Age 18, California

I HAVE OFTEN WONDERED WHERE I WOULD BE without the Latin Mass. I have often wondered whether I would still keep the Faith if I had not found it. Would I have kept it later into my adult years while my parents had a say in what I did and fallen away later, as so many people seem to do nowadays? Leaving the Catholic Church is a terrible thing to visualize, but really when I look back, I find that for a person such as I, there was very little other than God's grace—and perhaps a scrupulous conscience—to keep me from falling away. Of one thing I am certain though: I would never have come to love the Catholic Faith as much as I do now if it had not been for my discovering Tradition.

I will start at the beginning, with my first experience of the Latin Mass. My mother says our first TLM was at our local FSSP parish where my parents had enrolled me for Confirmation classes. They had chosen this somewhat-distant parish because they were uncomfortable with the preparation done at the diocesan level. Having seen how different things were not only in preparation for Confirmation but in everything ranging from how the people dressed to how the priests conducted themselves, we became curious to see what this different Mass was like. For years, they (especially my father) had been exasperated with all the liturgical abuse we saw at the Novus Ordo, and we had changed Mass times and places to encounter less of it. Dr. Peter Kwasniewski recently wrote in his Substack that, "Man is a 'tradition-constituted animal.'" Looking back on my family's journey towards Tradition, I can say that this is nothing but a true statement! We only knew as much as the average, mostly un-catechized Catholic does, yet we longed for something better: that reverence which in the end we could only find in the Tridentine Rite.

My first experience of the TLM, I am sad to say, was not as inspiring or beautiful as those of other people. First of all, I was quite shaken with how different everything was—not only the Mass in itself (which I obviously did not understand), but even the architecture. I do remember that, at first, I liked how reverent the liturgy was as a whole. But, having been a rather petty child, I later made up my mind that I had not liked it for a number of reasons, two of them being that it was different to what I was used to, and (probably) because it was too Catholic for me.

Like many people who have been raised in the post-Vatican II environment, I had the idea that being a Catholic meant little more than being excessively sentimental and wimpish. It also did not help that I grew up in a parish strongly influenced by the Charismatic movement, and that this group of Catholics was what I thought it meant to be "devout Catholics." I loathed it. I was not drawn to sentimentality when it came to the Faith. My greatest fear was that I would start to act like a Hispanic version of what in American Catholic circles nowadays is called a "Boomer Catholic". I guarded against any and most feelings or impulses of devotion which arose in me — and that was exactly what that first Latin Mass, along with the excellent, profound sermon of Our Lord's Passion, had awakened in me. Little did I know then that that first, small desire — that small, unwanted regret at past injuries against Our Lord, and that first Mass of the Ages — would be only the beginning of a long road down which I would come to love the Faith more fully.

As the years went by — but increasingly during and after the pandemic, when my exposure to the TLM increased — I fell completely in love with the Tridentine Rite. Nowadays, it is impossible for me to imagine what my life would be like without the Catholic Faith and without the Traditional Mass. I realize, in a way, that I would probably not be one without the other, because my soul was dying of starvation before I was fed the True, undiluted Faith through the Traditional Mass, the Mass of my ancestors and of so many saints and martyrs, who spilled their blood for this most precious of treasures, and for which I would gladly spill mine.

There are many reasons why I love the Latin Mass — so many, in fact, it would probably take me an entire book to examine them all in detail — but only one is its timeless beauty. The majestic beauty of the Tridentine Rite, along with its precious silence found nowhere else on earth, is simply heavenly. The lovely vestments worn by the priest, especially at the High Mass, are suggestive of royalty — and, appropriately so, for the Mass *is*, in the end, a royal affair, since Christ is King. Present at Mass, you are lost to time and the world while still being both in time and world, and for a moment you may take refuge away from cares, strife and noise, still ever and humanly conscious of them, but now in the solace provided for by the Mass of the Ages.

Another thing which I love is the order and preciseness with which the priest does everything. To me, this speaks of an inherent desire to please God by worshiping Him in as perfect a manner as possible. I must admit witnessing this aspect of the Mass is a particular joy to me, given I always wanted something more than the disorder commonly found in the Novus Ordo.

Lastly, the music used at the Tridentine Mass is something which I love deeply. Not only the Gregorian chant (of which I am very fond of), but also the "plain" organ music generally used for the Low Mass, which I usually attend. Having played the piano since Kindergarten, I have a keen sense when it comes to music. Whatever I listen to I am very conscious of, even unconsciously; or, in other words, music can have great meaning (or ruination) for me in whatever occasion I find it, which is why the sublime music of the organ influences me so greatly when I am present at Mass, and allows me to contemplate and pray better in ways that I could hardly explain, and that a dozen contemporary hymns expertly and relevantly composed never could. I have fallen so deeply in love with the organ, in fact, that I am now learning to play it, with hopes of being able to fulfill my years-long dream of playing at Mass someday.

The Traditional Mass has influenced my spiritual life greatly. Ever since I started attending, I have felt increasingly moved to want to please God more fully, something which I believe I would never have experienced otherwise. I have changed in ways I would never have conceived of. If you had asked me a few years ago where I would be now, I expect I would have replied with many things, but not with saying that my Catholic Faith would be as central to my life as it is now.

So, what does the Latin Mass mean to me? To me, the Latin Mass means everything. It is the most perfect expression of everything our Catholic Faith stands for and, it is, as Father Faber so rightly put it, "the most beautiful thing this side of Heaven." It is Heaven on earth itself, the place where those of us who are yet in exile in the world can experience, for a second, the bliss of Heaven. To this, I can only add these words, which echo those of so many who have found this Treasure of Treasures, our Mass: "Late have I loved you, O Beauty ever ancient and ever new! Late have I loved you!"

20. LOVE AND SACRIFICE: A BETROTHED COUPLE'S EXPERIENCE OF THE TLM
George & Jennifer, Age 24, Wisconsin

THE DECISION TO CELEBRATE OUR MARRIAGE with the Tridentine Mass is one not many understand. Friends, family, and co-workers all wonder: "Why would you do that?"; "What even is the Tridentine Mass?"; or "It isn't even in English, how are we supposed to understand?" In our mind, the Mass is not meant to be understood. That is not to say the Mass is without rhyme or reason—on the contrary, every part of the Mass serves its purpose within the context of the Mass. But the Mass is not something we can simply know; the Mass is a mystery of love and sacrifice.

Love and sacrifice are the foundations of a happy marriage. While paradoxical, it is through love and sacrifice that a couple achieves happiness in marriage. The Tridentine Mass exemplifies the duality of our salvation: love and sacrifice.

Every aspect of the Mass inspires and informs the Sacrifice of Our Lord on Calvary. The priest's gestures, kneeling, incense, silent prayers, and the like are real expressions of the Sacrifice of the Altar we are actively participating in at Mass. Our courtship and engagement centered around this form of sacrificial love: traveling far and wide—leaving the cozy and comfort of our university chapel—to celebrate the Mass according to the Ancient Rite. We put the Mass at the center of our relationship, sacrificing for each other to be present at the liturgy.

While our loved ones may not understand us, they do support us. We find great nourishment from friends and family, and enjoy being able to share our reasons for pursuing the Tridentine Mass. But those reasons occasionally prove insufficient in a world governed by sensational media headlines. At the same time, as we explain our love for the Mass, another article comes out detailing further restrictions on the Ancient Rite. These circumstances demand us, on the one hand, to defend the Church and, on the other hand, to act contrary to the supposed wishes of the Pope. The paradox is not lost on us.

The restrictions have demanded difficult decisions to be made regarding our celebration of marriage. Our home diocese maintains silent affirmation of the Tridentine Mass. Operating within the boundaries of the motu proprio *Traditionis Custodes*, our home diocese provides for a handful of Sunday morning Tridentine Masses. But beyond that, it exists in a liminal state of "Well, we don't know." It is, from our lay perspective, unclear if a nuptial Mass may be celebrated according to the ancient form. And no one wishes to confirm or deny that such may be had—silence is, after all, better than outright denial. At least for now.

Given these circumstances, we have had to make sacrifices. We cannot celebrate our wedding in the church where we first met. We cannot celebrate our wedding according to the Ancient Rite's nuptial Mass. We cannot fully share the nourishment of the liturgy with our loved ones. But through this sacrifice, we witnessed the charity and love shared between each other, and the charity and love others share with us.

Recognizing the transitional state of the Church, we find ourselves in, we pursued a difficult but ultimately beautiful solution: celebrate the Feast of Saints Peter and Paul immediately following our celebration of Christian marriage. While certainly not ideal, God most certainly willed this outcome. When we first discussed our eventual marriage, George stated he wanted to get married on the Feast of Saints Peter and Paul (St. Paul is the patron of the church where we first met). Providentially, the date was available at the church we will get married at. God, some years ago, guided us together. He then guided us to a certain day. And now He guides us to our unique solution to unfortunate circumstances. Were it not for our sacrifice, we do not believe our eyes and ears would have been open to God's will.

Through these sacrifices—and many others—our love has grown deeper for each other and for Christ. Our decisions do not make sense in the twenty-first century: waking up early to travel somewhere just for Mass? Putting Mass at the center of our Sundays? Having to work around the motu proprio when we could easily have a "reverent Novus Ordo?" While we certainly were not perfect in our dedication to the Tridentine Mass, it became the backbone of our relationship. Every day we could see in each other greater devotion and love for Christ. And within ourselves a greater desire to will the best for the other; a greater desire to achieve heaven for the other. Is heaven achievable without the Tridentine Mass? Of course. But our devotion to the Ancient Rite inspired a profound love of God and each other. For others in our life, this was nonsense. For us, it makes perfect sense.

Our desire to celebrate our marriage with the Tridentine Mass stems from our recognition that the Tridentine Mass highlights the sacrificial nature of the Mass. In our authentic pursuit of sainthood, sacrifice is necessary. Whether it is celebrating in a way strange to most, isolating ourselves in the eyes of our loved ones, or having to jump through bureaucratic hoops to celebrate this sacrament in a befitting way, we see these tribulations as small sacrifices preparing us for marriage.

21. A SUSPICIOUSLY GENUINE JOY
Breanna, Age 22, California

I WILL NEVER FORGET THE FIRST TIME I HEARD the beginning of the Asperges and the subsequent feeling of goosebumps on my arms. The priest walked down the aisle, sprinkling holy water on the laity, and it was not even Christmas or Easter. I did not know what was being sung, yet it was still the most beautiful thing I had ever heard in my life. I have always been a Catholic and have attended Mass at a variety of different parishes, but my first TLM was a culture shock to everything I had ever known about Catholicism. I remember thinking, "This is what going to a Catholic Mass is supposed to feel like."

I was born to a cradle Catholic mother and Protestant father, who would subsequently convert to the Faith when I was 3 years old. When my father first converted, my family became quite involved at our parish. But over time we would eventually attend Mass less often, to the point of maybe going on Christmas and Easter, if even Christmas and Easter. I think a passion for practicing the Faith and living it out was not present within my family. We did not value or understand the treasure we had, which is why it was so easy to drift away. We did not stop calling ourselves Catholic, but we would just pick out which practices we wanted to do now and then. During this time, my family just went with the flow. We lived like most other families and there was hardly anything about us that made us unique from the world.

By Divine Grace at one Easter morning Mass, my father realized that he needed to lead our family back to attending Mass and practicing the Faith regularly. We became very involved at our parish, coming to know many people as we volunteered at different events and attended Mass every Sunday. It did not take long for my family to become frustrated and confused with things that happened at Mass. My father would teach us about reverence and the universality of the Mass which would seem to be contradicted when we would attend our local Novus Ordo Mass.

Everyone always dressed casually, and the general morale was low. The reason these things bothered my family was because they did not align with everything we knew about Catholicism and the Mass. If we were attending the Marriage Supper of the Lamb, why was everyone dressed like they had just come from the beach? Why did Mass feel like an HOA meeting that we all had to attend? Why did everyone have these blank faces like we all did not really know why we did this every Sunday? Why were jokes being sprinkled throughout the Mass, with occasional antics involving props? Why was the music distracting from the liturgy rather than aiding it? Why did the focus seem to be on everything but the Eucharist? As a teen transitioning into a young adult, these were only a handful of the questions that I had.

As someone who loves to read, I loved reading about the Faith and became amazed with the saints' love for the Mass. They would arrive early to pray and prepare themselves to receive the Eucharist. I read about how they had a deep love for the Faith and cherished it like a treasure. I would become so excited to attend Mass and receive Jesus in the Eucharist at Mass. Despite this fire that would form in my heart to go to Mass and receive the Eucharist, I would sit in the pew and feel that fire slowly burn out. I told myself it was my fault. I was not a saint so I would not be able to understand their great love for the Mass and the Faith. The Mass was not about me so my love for it did not matter. I wondered if the Mass I attended every Sunday was the height of Catholicism. I thought about having to attend this same Mass every Sunday and wondered how I would grow spiritually if this was it.

Living in California during COVID lockdowns was both a blessing and a burden. Since everything was closed and we were all stuck at home, my family found ourselves occupied by learning more about the Faith through books and the Internet. During this time, my family began to learn about the topic of traditional Catholicism and the Traditional Latin Mass. The first main thing we learned about was receiving on the tongue. We had never thought about all the particles falling and being trampled upon, nor had we thought about how we were receiving the Lord with our unconsecrated hands. It did not take long for us to begin receiving on the tongue at our parish soon after. Our parish did not deny people the ability to receive the Eucharist in this way, but it sure did not make it a pleasant experience. My family would receive the Eucharist along with the taste of sanitizer as the person who would place our Lord upon our tongue had to sanitize each time someone received this way.

The irreverence during Mass only seemed to grow to a larger scale after the COVID lockdowns. This would lead my family to begin looking into the Traditional Latin Mass. I had not even heard about this Mass until my mid to late teens. From what I had heard, it was for strict, elderly people who liked the old way of doing things. This was not exactly appealing to me at the time, but my desperation for something other than what I was experiencing every Sunday at Mass was too great to be opposed to trying it out.

Believing the Traditional Latin Mass was something for serious, judgmental people, I struggled to find a dress that offered as much coverage as possible to avoid stern looks from surrounding attendees. I remember the first time I wore a veil for Mass, something about wearing it made me feel like I could dissolve into the crowd and be more focused on the Mass. There was so much to notice about the people entering the pews before Mass even started. My assumptions and preconceived notions about those who attended the Traditional Latin Mass were quickly erased as I saw something totally different from what I believed. Right away, I noticed everyone seemed happy. Everyone had this suspiciously genuine joy radiating from them. I thought, "Why are these people so happy? What is there to be so happy about?" Fellow Californians can understand this.

Another thing I noticed was how many young people there were. There were people around my age attending this Mass on their own. I do not think I knew of anyone at my old parish who was a young adult regularly attending on their own, at the very least, it was not common. There were families taking up entire pews and everyone was dressed appropriately. Previously, it was easy to fall into pride and arrogance because of all the rampant irreverence and disrespect displayed by people at Mass. For the first time, I felt humbled to be around people at Mass. Instead of looking outward, I was looking inward, at myself and any possible way I was displaying irreverence. As Mass began, I noticed how full the church was, which was another key difference from the Masses I was used to attending. The priest was not waving around to the congregation and shaking everyone's hand, but had his eyes cast downward, seemingly in a state of focus.

As the Asperges began, I felt something stir within my soul. My senses heightened and I began to hear the most beautiful words by the most beautiful voices I had ever heard, without understanding anything being said. I looked up toward the ceiling of the church and could imagine all of Heaven joining in with us in worship. Suddenly, everyone began to kneel. Why we were kneeling even though Mass had just begun, I did not know at the time. It was quiet and I could not hear anything the priest was saying, yet I realized I did not have to know everything he was saying at that moment. There were all these rituals of incensing and bowing and making the Sign of the Cross. I wondered why they did all these things and would scan through the side notes in my missal for explanations.

Everyone was focused on the Mass, and I got the sense that many people around me were filled with such pious devotion to what was taking place that I felt humbled to be worshiping alongside such devout Catholics. The hole in my heart was filled with such a fire for the Faith that it felt like nothing could extinguish it. I found what I was searching for at a place I did not know existed that long ago. I was witnessing a hidden treasure that I wanted everyone to know about. By the end of Mass, I felt like so many years of my life were robbed. I was robbed of my inheritance, which was the full truth and beauty of the Faith. I wondered how something so beautiful would not be taking place everywhere. Originally, my family planned to attend the TLM every first Sunday to have a break from the frustration of our home parish. After witnessing our first TLM together as a family, we unanimously knew there was no way we could only attend once a month, this Mass was too good, true, and beautiful to only attend 12 times a year.

With the unanimous understanding that we wanted to attend the TLM every Sunday, my family became stumped since we believed leaving our home parish would be akin to church shopping and we had become quite involved at the parish that our absence would be a damaging blow to the serious shortage of volunteers that aided at the Mass we attended. My father and brother would set up everything before Mass and clean up afterward. At the particular Mass we attended, no one liked helping with collection and there were practically no other consistent, dependable attendees to replace my father and brother, let alone help out during Mass.

As a young woman, I wished there were more men to help out my father and brother since I often had to help them with setting up, helping out during Mass, and cleaning up afterward. While I hold a special place in my heart for those times, I felt like I should not have had to do this. Where were the strong, Catholic men to take the lead? After going to the TLM, I knew the answer. My father, realizing he had a duty to raise his family in a parish that helped them grow closer to God, decided that our family needed to attend the TLM regularly and our time at our local parish had come to an end. After a series of awkward conversations with those at our old parish regarding our move to the TLM, the TLM parish finally became our home.

Since attending the TLM my spiritual life has transformed tremendously. I used to do just some basic prayers, and I did not have much of a routine. Becoming aware of other prayers and practices of the TLM inspired me to expand my prayer life and look into other devotions. The TLM exposed me to the reality of the supernatural, the connection between Heaven and Earth, and the Second Coming. This made me think more about my own sins and facing judgment for them, as well as my unforeseen death to come. These were things I did not think about often when I did not attend the TLM.

Above all, attending the TLM changed my perspective of the Eucharist. My love for the Blessed Sacrament skyrocketed and resulted in me realizing a need to attend confession more often, longing to attend Adoration for hours, and having a firmer belief in the Real Presence. There was something about the way everything was oriented toward the Eucharist, from the way we received our Lord to the way everyone gazed upon Him at the elevation. My love for the TLM stems from a longing for something consistent and unlike anything else in the world. I do not want to be catered to or given a watered-down version of the Faith. I want the truth given to me in its fullness and beauty. The TLM has fostered within me a sense of hope in a world that can appear to be hopeless. Seeing other young people like me having a similar passion for the TLM gives me hope that future generations will pass down the Faith of our ancestors, one that will lead to a flourishing community of faithful Catholics.

22. LIFE ON FIRE
Clare, Age 19, Tennessee

"When you sit in front of a fire in winter, you are just there in front of the fire. You don't have to be smart or anything. The fire warms you." This quote by Desmond Tutu explains how I feel about the Latin Mass. For me the Latin Mass feels like a roaring fire in a snowy clearing in a forest. After being lost in the forest of the world during the week I can draw close to the warm fire of the Latin Mass, and it brings comfort to my soul. As the quote says, "You don't have to be smart or anything. The fire warms you." This is how I see the Latin Mass. Yes, it is in a language that we don't understand, but it is still the Mass and God is in the Mass and so anyone who goes to Latin Mass still gets the same benefits of going to a Novus Ordo Mass. In my opinion, the Latin Mass being in another language gives a person the opportunity to meditate more on the Mass and different aspects of Catholic teaching.

As I was growing up, a religious order called Miles Christi, which is Latin for Soldier of Christ, established themselves about an hour away from where I lived in Michigan. The Miles Christi religious order is based in Argentina and has expanded their order to Michigan and California, as well as Colorado. Their order is based on Ignatian spirituality, and their most predominant focus is on families and young adults, which my family was a part of for many years. At all of Miles Christi's Masses they used the Novus Ordo, but they also used many aspects of the Latin Mass, this is what kickstarted my family's journey with the Latin Mass. Miles Christi exposed my family to a concept of our Catholic faith that seemed so foreign at first, but then we grew to love it because of how spiritually deep it felt.

I mostly grew up on the Latin Mass, the first parish I went to that celebrated the Latin mass was All Saints Catholic Church in Flint, MI. My older brother started serving the Latin Mass at this parish and went on to become a Master of Ceremonies. When that parish closed, my family and I went to St. Matthew's Catholic Church in Flint, which is where I first started singing in the choir. A year ago, I moved to East Tennessee and now attend St. Mary's Catholic Church. For the Latin Mass, I don't have to understand the language or know what is going on, all I know is that I am praising God. I find it fascinating that ecclesiastical Latin, though it is considered a dead language, is the language that the evil one fears the most.

I've always loved the Latin Mass. Sure, when I was little, when the cantor was chanting, I thought that the cantor was going on and on just to make the mass longer and to make me suffer more in my little kid-ness. Though, as I grew up and eventually joined the choir, I grew to love Gregorian chant. The chant and music that I learned from my first Latin Mass choir director, a man from Czechoslovakia, was what made me fall in love with the Latin Mass. Singing for the Latin Mass always made me feel like I was singing with the angels before the throne of God. Singing for mass also helped me know my vocal range better and pushed my voice to the limits I did not know I could go to. Overall, the music of the Latin Mass was a big part of why I love it, but that's not all of why I love the Latin Mass.

The Latin Mass requires you to engage in mental prayer especially during the Low Mass. The Latin Mass can be said in two different ways, the High Mass or the Low Mass. A High Mass has more cantoring and responding whereas the Low Mass is mostly just the priest and servers saying the Mass while the congregation prays and participates quietly. One thing I like to do during a Low Mass is to meditate on the Introit for that day. It allows me to enter more fully into the worship of God. I took Latin classes in high school, I can't write or speak it, but I can read it and sing it so during the Mass I also like to follow along with the missalette that has what the priest is saying, and it allows me to learn more Latin as well as follow along with the priest. Peter Kwasniewski once said, "If you want a church full of Catholics who know their faith, love their faith and practice their faith, give them a liturgy that is demanding, profound and rigorous. They will rise to the challenge." This is another reason why I love the Latin Mass because it is demanding, profound and rigorous. The Latin Mass is both rigorous and demanding and these two aspects go hand in hand. It is rigorous because it demands one's full attention unlike my experience with the Novus Ordo where I find myself more easily distracted. In the Latin Mass, the priest faces away from the people, symbolically pointing to Christ, which is where my full attention should be. It is profound because everything done and said within the Latin Mass has a deep meaning to it. Nothing is done casually. I love how much the Latin mass requires of me as well as encouraging me to keep learning what I can about my faith.

Another aspect that draws me to the TLM, is the community that we have always found there. No matter where we go to Latin Mass, we always find so many young families and young adults. People are always surprised when I tell them this because they think that the Latin Mass wouldn't be attractive to young people. However, I have always found the opposite to be true. Some of my best friends are young people that I have met through the Latin Mass. Not only do I find the future of the church in the people at the Latin Mass, but I also find that many people at the Latin Mass have many things that are needed for the future of the church to thrive. Some of these things are a deeper faith, vocations to the religious life and priesthood as well as self-sacrifice in which they help either the parish or the church community with whatever is needed whether it be in their personal lives or for a community event.

For many people the Latin Mass might seem weird or a little radical, but that is only because they either haven't experienced it for themselves or they did not have an open heart to what the Latin Mass could offer them. For me the saying "Lex orandi, lex vivendi." How you pray impacts how you live," gives me that meaning of how the Latin Mass affects me. For me, ever since I started really understanding how beautiful and impactful the Latin Mass was for me it has impacted how I see and care about the world. I'm not saying that the only way to get things done or the only way to pray is by going to Latin Mass. I'm saying that because of the Latin Mass I have found something impactful and encouraging for my soul and it has given me a reason to continue learning more about my faith and to continue practicing it as well.

In conclusion, I love the Latin Mass because it gives my heart a burning desire for God more than anything else could ever give me. For someone to start going to the Latin Mass I would recommend trying to follow along in the missalette, but if that gets too hard, start just meditating on God, Heaven, angels, the crucifixion or the Last Supper. Don't think too hard about if you're doing something wrong, most likely there are other people just like you who don't know what to do as well, just let the words that are said pull you into their power and wonder. The Latin Mass is the Novus Ordo but with much more depth and meaning because it has been said for many centuries and generation upon generation have participated in its depth. I grew up on the Latin Mass but I didn't understand the need for going to Mass until very recently. This gave me the initiative to really focus on God and my relationship with him.

23. TO UNDERSTAND THE REAL MEANING OF SACRIFICE
Dominic, Age 15, Michigan

"MARTYRDOM IS NOTHING IN COMPARISON with the Mass, because martyrdom is the sacrifice of man to God, whereas the Mass is the Sacrifice of God for man!" This quote by Saint John Vianney expresses the greatness of the Holy Sacrifice of the Mass. St. John Vianney was known for celebrating the Mass with great reverence and devotion. He lived in a time when all priests said the Mass in Latin and the ceremonies were very elaborate. The Mass that was said in his time is commonly known today as the Latin Mass or the Extraordinary Form. It has commonly been asked why someone would want to go to a Latin Mass when they could just as easily go to a Mass said in their mother tongue or one that is much shorter. I am attracted to the Latin Mass because it is contemplative, is sacrificial, and has helped me to understand the real meaning of sacrifice and to see other forms of sacrifice in my daily life.

The Latin Mass is contemplative and allows for verbal and mental prayer. The atmosphere of the Mass, with the chanting, music, and quiet prayers of the priest, makes it very easy for me to pray mentally. The chanting helps me to pray mentally by helping me to focus, direct my thoughts to prayer, and to keep from distraction. The music helps me to pray by subduing all the background noise in the church and redirecting my thoughts if my mind strays from praying. When the priest is quietly praying the prayers of the Mass, I can turn to mental prayer and do not have to focus on necessarily making the responses. Besides being contemplative, it is also sacrificial.

By saying the Latin Mass is sacrificial, I am not saying that the Novus Ordo is not a sacrifice to God for our sins, I am merely saying that the Latin Mass provides opportunities for me to offer up my discomfort and hard work to God more easily than in the Novus Ordo. It allows this in two different ways: the discomfort of not being able to understand what the priest is sometimes saying, and the hard work and sacrifice that was required of me to learn to serve the Latin Mass. The discomfort of not being able to understand what the priest is sometimes saying, gives me the opportunity to offer this discomfort up to God and allows me to enter more into praying the Sacrifice of the Mass, this further allows me to deepen my prayer.

The hard work and sacrifice that was required of me to learn to serve the Latin Mass, has allowed me to enter into the liturgy more by offering up to God not only what I have learned with his help, but also the perseverance and hard work that God gave me to learn it. When I was learning to serve, I not only had to learn things like when to bring the cruets to the priest, when to ring the bells, and how to carry a candle et cetera, I also had to memorize prayers and responses in a different language. As an altar server, I also rely on verbal cues to tell me when to perform certain duties.

When I learned to serve the Latin Mass, I had to start fresh, learn, and pay careful attention to what the priest said when certain duties were performed, so that I would know when to perform them. It took me about two years before I was able to completely master serving. All this hard work, I did, and still do, I offer up to God. I enter more deeply into praying the Sacrifice of the Mass, by offering up to God all the work that I have put into learning to serve the Latin Mass, and by offering back to God the talent he has given me. The Latin Mass is contemplative and sacrificial, but it has also taught me much.

The Latin Mass has taught me to see the real meaning of sacrifice and to see other forms of sacrifice in my life, particularly in my effort to learn the technique of Byzantine icon writing. It has taught me to see sacrifice as not just what is offered, but what it takes to get there. The Latin Mass has taught me, in my effort to learn how to write Byzantine icons, that I am offering to God not only the fruit of my labors, the icon, but also the labor, perseverance, craftsmanship, and money that it took to write the icon. The process that it takes to write an icon is very long, tedious, and laborious, very much like the process of learning to serve the Mass. It requires the use of many expensive materials. It requires long hours of practice in many different skills. The process used to write an icon can take weeks. In all of this, the Latin Mass has taught me that it is all a sacrifice and an offering to God. It has taught me that sacrifice is not just what is physically offered, but also the journey of acquiring the physical offering.

You can clearly see why I am attracted to the Latin Mass, and what I have learned from it. The contemplative atmosphere allows me to enter deeper into prayer. The sacrificial nature of the Mass has taught me that sacrifice is not only the fruit of the labor, but also the labor itself. The Latin Mass has taught me, in my effort to learn how to write Byzantine icons, that I am offering to God, not just the icon, but also everything that went into writing the icon, and that all of this is a sacrifice. It has helped me to grow and deepen my spiritual life greatly. I hope that people will, despite the Latin Mass being long, rigorous, and in a different language, give it a try.

24. THE CURE THIS WORLD IS IN DIRE NEED OF
Sofia, Age 15, Texas

I FIRST WAS INTRODUCED TO THE TRADITIONAL Latin Mass when I began attending my current school; we start the day off by attending Mass. At first, I was distraught by the differences between this somewhat estranged Mass and the Novus Ordo, but I soon came to understand it and grew a deep love for it. It has now been a full year that I have devoutly attended the TLM at my school, and I fully intend to continue to faithfully attend until the end of my days.

I was always disturbed by how irreverent certain aspects of the Novus Ordo were. I attempted to just turn a blind eye, work on myself being reverent and not pay any haste to those around me; yet it still bothered me. There were so many things, whether large or small of matter, that just didn't sit right with me: such as receiving communion in the hand, female altar servers, Eucharistic ministers, lectors, standing when receiving communion, the entire altar facing us, and so, so much more. I couldn't help but think, "Why might it be this way? Why out of all things, is the holy sacrifice of the Mass so disrespectful?" Going to the TLM has helped me to see that it doesn't need to be, that it shouldn't be.

I was always scared to discuss my faith with fellow brothers and sisters in Christ, for I knew that, though we both may be Catholic, we might not share the exact same beliefs. Once at my previous school, I accidentally mentioned something I had thought to be common sense, and was scorned by my entire classroom, including the teacher. So, when I was surrounded by like-minded people within the TLM community, I was ecstatic and eager to debate. To this day I still remember the relief I had to know that there were people with whom I could relate to, people I could go to with matters of the faith without having to be concerned that they might ridicule my ideals.

I have always thought Latin to be a beautiful language, it is the language the church first went by, and the language feared by the devil himself. St. Augustine says, "The one who sings prays twice." And the sung Latin prayers are so beautiful they make me want to cry. After Mass we regularly sing the Salve Regina as they process out and I can honestly say that nothing sounds quite like it. I have only had the pleasure of participating in a solemn high sung Mass a few times, and what I love about it is not the theatrics, but the heartfelt care that goes into it. You can feel the entire congregation praying with such devotion and faith, and I feel as if my own soul is lifted by the angels delivering these profoundly faithful prayers up to our Lord. And I do understand that the Novus Ordo has sung Masses too, but they just aren't as powerful.

I now find myself in a position where it is harder for me to be able to attend the traditional liturgy, and I yearn for it; I have a desire which the Novus Ordo cannot fulfill. The Traditional Latin Mass has gotten me through a lot of rough patches, and I know it will help heal all of the scars I hide, all the trauma I attempt to leave behind me, and help me to carry all of the burdens which lay heavy upon my shoulders.

The traditional liturgy has helped me grow in my faith more than I could have ever imagined, I've learned things I never even thought to ask. I can only pray that many others may be able to experience what I have, and that many others pass their knowledge of the faith to people going through the same thing. I am now in the closest and most intimate relationship with our Lord and savior Jesus Christ than I ever have been, and it is all thanks to the traditional liturgy. The TLM means the world to me, I have openly invited all of my friends to join me on any given Sunday so they may see the true splendor of it, and I will continue to do so for as long as I live.

The Traditional Latin Mass is not only the true Mass of the church, but it is the only thing that may be able to melt the ice-cold heart of the people in this world today. Help them to see that the Traditional Liturgy is not backwards, and that, in truth, the Novus Ordo is actually the one that is backwards. Pope Leo XIII had a vision, some say that it was of a conversation between God and Satan, saying he needed only a hundred years, and he would destroy the church; and others say it was of our current generation, of all that happens in this time. No matter what it was, it was centered about these times, and it filled him with enough fear to create an entire prayer to prevent it from coming to pass and had it said every day for years on end. We are now living in those times and, we do not know just how bad it could have been, but the Catholic faith still is not sitting pretty. So many people are sickened at the prospect of the Catholic Church, and many of our brothers and sisters are shying away and not standing up for what they believe in. Well, I believe that the only thing that may be able to help is the Traditional Latin Mass, I believe that it is the cure that the world is in dire need of.

The TLM is under attack, and it is asking us to protect it. Many are accusing it of being far too old school and outdated, they don't see the beauty in it. Pope Pius XII taught us that the sacred liturgy is intimately intertwined with the truths of the Catholic faith, and that we therefore must accept, and reflect these truths in our daily lives. I hear the call and am willing to pick up my cross and aid in the protection of the Traditional Latin Mass. Are you?

25. THE BEAUTIFUL POETRY OF LATIN
Joseph, Age 17, Michigan

THE GREATEST GIFT GOD HAS GIVEN US IS HIS life. When Christ was crucified, he gave up his life so that we all could live with him in eternity. The mass is the renewal of His sacrifice. Every time the mass is celebrated it is a sacrifice of Christ's love for us. The mass is the center of the Church's life; it gives us the Body, Blood, Soul, and Divinity of Jesus Christ. It is the pinnacle of a Catholic's life.

Latin has always been and still is the universal language of the Church so what better way to celebrate the mass than in the tongue of the Church itself. I have studied Latin for over six years and during that time I have come to not only learn the language but appreciate it as a beautiful and poetic language. The way the vowels and syllables come together to form words that give it a sense of rhythm and harmony. It is a dead language, yes, in the sense that it is not used by people to communicate *en masse*. To me however, it is more alive than ever within the Latin mass.

The mass itself is beautiful and when combined with the Latin language it creates a whole new beauty. The sacrifice of Christ is embodied through the Latin language. When the hymns are sung or when the many readings and psalms are chanted in the Latin language, it creates a prayerful atmosphere. While I know Latin to a certain extent, sometimes I do not understand what is being said, but I find that to be a good thing. My reasoning for this is that sometimes we may be so intent on listening to what is being said out loud, that we miss what God is trying to tell us silently. So, when the Latin words are being chanted the meaning is there as it would be in another language, but by not truly understanding each phrase it gives you a chance to pray to yourself, but still with a prayerful atmosphere in the background. Creation is a mystery, God is a mystery, and the mass is a mystery. So why not allow the words to be a mystery, but still with meaning. Just as we have faith in God even though we sometimes do not understand his reasoning. This in itself shows to me that the Latin language and the mass are truly a perfect pair.

Just as the mass and Latin mirror God and his reasoning, so does each motion of the mass. The Latin Mass is not just chanting and singing Latin, it is also a motion. Each movement the priest and servers make is made for a reason. For example, when the missal, used during the mass, is moved from one side to the other, that is a representation that the Jews were first preached to, but after their rejection of it was preached to the Gentiles. Another very small but powerful motion is that almost everything is spoken or done in threes, not once or twice, but always three times. At every incensation it is always done with three swings. The *Domine non sum dignus* is recited three times. At one movement in the mass the servers perform an action which includes genuflecting three times. During the mass the water and wine are each used three times. These are small things that many might not notice, but they are there as a constant symbolism of the Trinity.

As we all know the mass originates from the Last Supper where Christ instituted the Eucharist. The mass we know today is not what the Last Supper was almost two thousand years ago. Those two thousand years are responsible for the slow change to what we know today as the Mass. In the early days of the Christians the Last Supper was celebrated in a different way, but to an extent it had the same basic structure of what the mass is today. There is an excerpt from Saint Justin the Martyr where he describes the mass and gives details of its celebration. In his excerpt he talks of how the mass was celebrated on Sundays, the day Jesus rose from the dead. This is still true to this day. We still go to mass each Sunday, but we also have daily mass now which is a welcome change from then. There were readings from the apostles and prophets, which was followed by instruction from the president as Justin says or in other words the priest. This was followed by the breaking of bread and as we know it today, the consecration. Each community had their own way of celebrating the mass, but they all had the same basic structure. Those communities became the different rites such as the Latin rite, the Byzantine rite, the Chaldean rite, and many others. The mass we know today is what once was the Christian communities of Rome and other Latin speaking communities. The Latin Mass does not just use Latin as a language for no reason. It is used because of generations passing down that language with the mass. Even as the centuries changed the world and people, the Latin mass stayed the same. So, the Latin mass also carries a rich history with it. Each generation added small things and customs to the Latin mass. The prayers and movements did not just come from nowhere. So, each time the Latin Mass is celebrated, it was generations of priests, religious, and laity that made the Latin Mass prayerful and beautiful. It is a reminder that we are all one in the body of Christ, the Church. It is a reminder that death is not the end. Hundreds of years of people made the Latin mass what it is today. Even we ourselves are adding to the mass, though not at every mass, but at many it has become customary to recite the Saint Michael's prayer at the end of the Mass. That is how and why the Latin mass is so beautiful and prayerful today. Each generation added very little things, but hundreds of generations of people can and did create something beautiful.

The Latin mass is a beautiful celebration of Christ's death and resurrection. Each part of the mass leads us to prayer and thoughtfulness in Christ. The movements of each part give symbolism and meaning to the mass. The music and chanting of hymns give the mass a prayerful atmosphere. All of it is constructed in a way that leads you to Christ. It was the work of hundreds of years of Catholics adding something to what once was the Last Supper and now is the beautiful and wondrous Latin Mass of today. Pax Domini sit semper vobiscum.

26. THE MYSTERY BEFORE WHICH ONE TREMBLES
Audro, Age 23, Singapore

In "The Glory of the Lord", von Balthasar remarked that "beauty is the disinterested one, without which the ancient world refused to understand itself, a word which both imperceptibly and yet unmistakably has bid farewell to our new world, a world of interested, leaving to its own avarice and sadness." This profound observation about beauty's disappearance sets the stage for an examination of the modern world—a world, I contend, that has largely turned its back on the transcendence of beauty. Despite the pressures of post-modernity, the Catholic Church calls us to live out our faith in the world, a challenge we find difficult to embrace. Yet, in the stark and bleak landscape of modernity, the Traditional Mass emerges as a luminous beacon of beauty, a direct reflection of the divine. It is not merely the aesthetics—the enchanting solemn tone of Gregorian chant, the rich and fragrant scent of incense or the intricate beauty of the liturgical vestments—that draw me repeatedly to the Traditional Mass. Rather, it is the profound sense of encountering something eternal and transcendent that pulls at the soul, offering a glimpse of heavenly realities amidst the earthly. It makes one feel deeply what Newman said as a boy: "I thought life might be a dream, or I an Angel, and all this world a deception". It teaches us how real heavenly realities are and how transient and shadowy this visible world of ours is. As you read this essay, please understand that my narrative may seem disjointed, reflecting my own ongoing journey. This is not just a tale of aesthetic appreciation but an account of one's faith, of beauty interwoven with life's fabric. Here, I endeavour to share how the Mass, with its timeless ritual, continues to shape my understanding of beauty and faith, marking crucial waypoints in my spiritual journey.

Growing up in the technocratic milieu of Singapore, I often found myself immersed in a utilitarian ethos, which seeped even into the realm of worship. As a child, my religious life consisted of perfunctory attendance at Sunday Masses—more a routine of familial obedience than an act of religion. The liturgical landscape I encountered was that of the typical Novus Ordo, which, despite its dizzying number of options, seemed to gravitate towards the lowest common denominator bereft of a sacred atmosphere. This, coupled with my lack of catechesis, made the Mass feel spiritually empty and useless and I longed for the day when I could finally stop going to Mass.

It was only later, at the age of 15, that I came under the influence of Joseph Ratzinger and St. Thomas Aquinas. This intellectual awakening initiated a process of humility, revealing the beautiful consistency in the perennial teachings and intellectual patrimony of the Church. This newfound sense of "consonantia" which I found in reading philosophy and theology stood in stark contrast to my lived liturgical experience. The disjunction between intellectual assent to the doctrine of Transubstantiation and its internalisation at the point of the reception of Holy Communion is particularly dire. The musical accompaniment, more redolent of puerile entertainment than sacred hymnody, served to obfuscate this tremendous reality of the presence of the King of Kings. Providentially, by this time, *Summorum Pontificum* had been promulgated for which I will always remain grateful to Ratzinger.

My first encounter with the traditional Mass is akin to what I found when I first began to read the descriptions of beauty in the *Summa* of St Thomas: "integritas", "consonantia", and "claritas." It was clear from the first moment that it was a rite of utmost gravity and solemnity dedicated to one thing and one thing only, the worship of God. To appropriate Kierkegaard's definition of a saint as the capacity to "will the one thing," I can attest that from the first moment of attending the Traditional Mass, I was captivated by an overwhelming sense of the sacred, what Rudolf Otto calls the "mysterium tremendum et fascinans," the mystery before which one trembles in awe and yet is irresistibly drawn towards. Since that transformative moment, my reverence for and attachment to the traditional Roman rite has only deepened, echoing Ratzinger's assertion that the liturgy cannot be created ex nihilo. The traditional Mass continues to be for me a wellspring of spiritual nourishment.

It would be mistaken to attribute my attachment to the traditional Mass to mere aestheticism or some sort of yearning for a bygone era of Catholicism. Born at the turn of the millennium, I find myself in the position of being considered excessively "traditional" by mainstream Catholic standards, yet too liberal for many traditionalists. For example, I am not opposed, in principle, to vernacular readings. My reservations about the revised offertory prayers are tempered by an awareness of the historical diversity in liturgical practice, as evidenced in the rites of religious orders and ancient sacramentaries. I also believe that the Roman Rite, while venerable, is not immutable. The Second Vatican Council's call for liturgical renewal, as articulated in *Sacrosanctum Concilium*, was a much-needed expression of the Church's ability to adapt and revise her forms of worship. However, I concur with priests like Fr. Robert McTeigue, S. J., who claims that the implementation of these reforms often diverged from the Council's original intent. My attraction to the Mass is then fundamentally rooted in its capacity to fulfil the psalmist's exhortation to "worship the LORD in the beauty of holiness" (Psalm 96:9).

While acknowledging the inherent sanctity of the Pauline Rite, its celebration frequently lacks the "noble simplicity" called for by the Council, often veering instead towards banality that fails to elevate the soul. As T. S. Eliot observed, "The communication of the dead is tongued with fire beyond the language of the living." The traditional Roman rite, in its organic development over millennia, embodies this "communication of the dead," offering a profound connection to the historical and cultural roots of Western civilization. I have gained insights into the intricate tapestry of Western culture —its architecture, music, and art —far surpassing what could be gleaned through academic study alone through my immersion in the pure waters of the traditional liturgy. This somewhat mirrors Newman's idea of "real assent," where truth is not merely intellectually apprehended but personally experienced. The Mass, in its multifaceted richness, is also for me a font of spiritual and cultural enlightenment, a living embodiment of the faith passed down through the ages.

The traditional Mass, in its profound embodiment of what Pelikan calls "the living faith of the dead," serves as a locus of anamnesis—a remembrance that makes present the entirety of salvation history. This concept finds its fullest expression in the rich symbolism and ritual of the Mass. As is said in *Sacrosanctum Concilium*, "The liturgy is the summit toward which the activity of the Church is directed; it is also the font from which all her power flows." This power, I contend, stems from the capacity of the Mass to effect what can only be described as a double constellation of the true and the good, manifested through beauty. The Mass, in its traditional form, embodies a sacramental ontology that reveals the world as a sign pointing to God. It is, to borrow from Henri de Lubac, not merely a ritual but the very action that "makes the Church." My experience of the Mass has been a gradual awakening to this reality—a realisation that in participating in this ancient rite, I am engaging in an act of cosmic significance that transcends time and space. Liturgy, as a set form of worship, is not something that we make, but something that transforms us. This transformation occurs through what the Orthodox priest Alexander Schmemann calls "the sacrament of the kingdom," where the earthly liturgy becomes a participation in the heavenly liturgy.

The beauty of the Mass, far from being mere aestheticism, serves a profoundly theological purpose. Von Balthasar argues in *The Glory of the Lord* that "Beauty is the last thing which the thinking intellect dares to approach, since only it dances as an uncontained splendour around the double constellation of the true and the good and their inseparable relation to one another." In the traditional Mass, this beauty becomes a gateway to the divine, drawing the worshipper into a deeper contemplation of the mysteries of the Faith.

In the final analysis, Dostoevsky's profound assertion that "beauty will save the world" is especially true when discussing the liturgy. In the liturgy, it is not a mere aesthetic indulgence but a path by which we might glimpse the splendour of eternal truths amidst the transience of our earthly existence. Again, I quote Dostoevsky that "without beauty, [man] could no longer live." The traditional Mass, in its rich symbolism and timeless ritual, offers this essential spiritual sustenance. My own experience is simply an anecdote, but it is one of many that points to the enduring power of the liturgy to shape and transform the soul, echoing Cardinal Newman's reflection that "to live is to change, and to be perfect is to have changed often."

Yet, this change is not a rupture with the past but a deepening of our connection to it. The traditional Mass, as a living link to centuries of faith and culture, offers a unique synthesis of continuity and renewal. It is, to borrow from Gustav Mahler, a way of "preserving the fire, not the ashes" of our tradition. As I continue to attend the traditional Mass, I am ever more convinced of its capacity to elevate the human spirit and orient it towards the transcendent. The traditional Mass stands as a refuge, offering all who would come that "beauty ever ancient, ever new" of which St. Augustine spoke.

27. THE BIG CROSSOVER
Abraham, Age 12, Delaware

At our church, there are little red booklets that have the Latin text of the Traditional Latin Mass on one side, and the English translation on the other. There are also short notes throughout the text that explain certain parts. One Sunday, when I was about six years old, I was following along the best I could, when I read the note that the priest makes the Sign of the Cross fifty-two times during the course of the Mass. Although I was very young at the time, that detail really stood out to me, and struck me as very significant: a relatively small, but powerful and important gesture, made a very specific number of times.

This characteristic of the Latin Mass—the attention to small details, the precision with which words and gestures are performed, the significance of every motion—is one that has continued to make a deep impression on me. I have been attending the Traditional Latin Mass a few times a month since I was born, but it was after I received my First Communion, when I began learning to serve, that I really began to appreciate so many of these small details.

Nothing at the Latin Mass happens by accident or is left to chance. Every movement that the altar servers make is made deliberately, in a particular way. For example, one of the first things I was taught when I began serving was how to do what my instructor called, "the big crossover." When the priest closes the Tabernacle door after Communion, the servers rise, move to the center, genuflect, turn ninety degrees, and walk to the far ends of the altar. They then walk at the same time up each side of the steps; the server on the left picks up the book, and the server on the right picks up the chalice veil. They both bow to the altar, walk down their respective steps, and genuflect in the middle. The server with the missal rises, and climbs the steps on the right side, and replaces the missal on the altar. Meanwhile, the server with the veil walks up the left steps and assists the priest with the burse and veil. Then both come down the steps, genuflect together, and kneel in their places.

Learning how to do this movement correctly was a very important step in our training. Although on the surface the process seems like a simple "switch," each of these movements is done as symmetrically as possible; the servers move carefully and reverently with no unnecessary gestures or movements. When the altar servers are not doing an active job, they stand, sit, or kneel at attention in a very particular way, keeping their hands pressed together in front of their chests. If seated, they keep their backs straights and their palms resting on their knees. In this way, their very posture helps to show reverence to the Lord, but it doesn't draw any unnecessary attention to themselves, which might distract the people at Mass from their worship of God.

The priest, similarly, moves in a very deliberate manner throughout the Mass. His motions and gestures are specified by the rubrics of the Mass, and he does not omit or add anything to what is written down. All of this has one purpose: to maintain everyone's focus on the task at hand, which is worshipping God, giving Him the respect and reverence, He deserves.

This attitude and atmosphere of reverence generally applies to the people in the pews as well. Although there are no rules directing exactly what the people are to do during the Mass, their behavior and dress at the Latin Mass is generally very reserved and professional. They have clearly come here to do something specific. There is a feeling that we are all engaged in doing something very, very important.

Adding to that sense of importance is the use of the Latin language itself. Because this is a language, we do not use anywhere else, it helps to reinforce the distinctiveness of what we are doing at the Mass. Hearing the prayers in this special language helps to remove us from our everyday world and place us in the presence of God and His saints. One of my favorite aspects of this is the way that, perhaps due to the unique architecture at my parish church, when some of the shorter prayers are chanted at top of the altar, the syllables echo, and almost hang suspended in air, like the clouds of incense. In these moments, there is a brief, but unmistakable, feeling of otherworldliness.

Some people might think that all this attention to detail, all this formality, is strange and unnecessary. It seems different from the way the rest of the world works. Most people assume that young people want things to be casual and easy. Learning all the responses in Latin, especially the Confiteor, is certainly not easy! Memorizing the correct movements, paying vigilant attention to what needs to be done when, is not easy, either.

However, there are many times even in secular life when people are motivated to do things that are hard or uncomfortable. For example, people put a lot of effort into activities like sports or scouting.

People will push themselves to run faster or throw harder to perform at their best level in baseball. They wear an uncomfortable uniform on hot days and play hours-long games in competitive tournaments. In scouting, young people challenge themselves to do difficult projects, hike up mountains, and carry heavy packs; they wear a formal uniform and participate in highly scripted civic ceremonies. People put effort into these activities because they think they are important. Yet, while these are worthy activities, their significance pales in comparison to the importance of worshipping God.

The precision of the words and gestures, the dress and comportment of the priest and servers, the solemn attendance of the people in the pews, the use of a set-apart language, all send a message. If even a nonreligious person walked into a church during a Latin Mass, he would be able to tell that something very important and special was happening. The fact that we are worshipping God is very apparent at the Latin Mass.

It might seem that worship should be something easy, but it is actually often quite difficult. We need all the help we can get to worship properly.

This is what makes the Latin Mass so special: it gives us that help, in abundance. While any valid Mass is of infinite value, the Traditional Latin Mass conveys that to me in a very concrete, unmistakable way, and helps me to worship God in the way He deserves.

28. "RAPID GROWTH IN MY SPIRITUAL LIFE"
Prosper, Age 22, Nigeria

I HAVE ASKED MYSELF A COUPLE OF TIMES recently what the Traditional Latin Mass means to me and I realized to my greatest surprise that I have never really thought about it anytime in the past, I mean since 2021 when I started assisting at the TLM, the subject has never crossed my thought—well, not until recently. Things are looking different now that I have assiduously thought about it, and I am happy that I did because it really opened my eyes to notice things that I did not know were there and now I will proceed to share "the fruits of my contemplation" as St. Bernard instructed his brothers. This essay will cover three sections, the first section describing how I discovered the TLM, the next section will talk about the benefits the Mass has availed me, and finally I am going to tell the world what the TLM means to me. Let's dig in!

I was admitted into the Federal University of Technology Owerri in December of 2019 to study a 5-year course in Mechanical Engineering, and this is where my story begins. A few months after my Matriculation in March of 2020, COVID struck and for 8 months, I was at home. Everything was literally shut down, no one could move around and for someone about my age here in Nigeria, there was absolutely nothing to do, except for social media. I simply kept myself busy all day on Facebook and it was there that I met a guy who actually turned out to be my course mate in school and sooner than you know it we were already friends. Fast-forward to 8 months later when school finally resumed, we met physically, and we became best buddies, and I will always go and visit him in the school dormitory where he was staying at that time (I was staying off-campus) and I will spend almost all my free time there to the extent that his roommates started seeing me as one of them. On one fateful day, I visited him as usual but he was cooking and so I laid down on his bed reading Dan Brown's *Inferno* with my back on the bed and the book suspended in the air by my two arms. Few minutes later, his roommate, Leonard, brushed past me, and he noticed the book I was reading and stopped and told me that it wasn't a good book and that it would mess with my faith (which was actually true but I had not realized at the time) but I firmly told him that I would need more than *Inferno* to shake my faith, and he left me but he never gave up on me. I had met my God-sent angel, and I knew it not.

Day after day, when I would visit my friend, Leonard would invite us Catholics in the rooms to say Angelus at 12PM and after the prayers, he would dismiss us and continue with the Little Office of the Immaculate Conception of the Blessed Virgin Mary alone. Day after day, as I see him say his prayers when no one else does, my admiration for him grew and soon enough, I started joining him for the Office and that is how we started talking and we became good friends till date. On a very good day, Leo invited me to come to Mass with him but the Mass he described was very different from the one I knew. I can still remember when he said that there was a Holy Water font where you dip your hands and make the Sign of the Cross afterwards. I promised to go with him but the day I would go, I was not certain. At that time, I was a lector in the chaplaincy in school and so my Sundays were not usually free, but Leo never gave up, he kept on reminding me and I kept stalling but on one fateful Sunday, on 6th of June 2021, I went with him and for the first time I assisted at the TLM, I was 19 at the time. It was a 70-minute journey, but we arrived just in time for the Mass. Everything Leo described was as I had pictured it except for the Holy Water font. Honestly, I had imagined that the font would actually be like the ones you see in the movies adorning the great palaces of Europe and the streets of Rome and so I was quite disappointed. There was Confession before the Mass, which was strange to me because in the Novus Ordo where I was brought up, it was actually abnormal nay, even forbidden to have Confessions on Sundays.

Then came the High Mass. A lot of things about it was confusing, I hardly understood the priest's sermon because it was too fast for my comprehension, the many Signs of the Cross was weird, everyone was standing and sitting and kneeling at odd intervals but the few things that impressed me was, first, the live flowers on the Altar, second, the whole Mass was in Latin which was good for me because even as a kid I had always preferred the Mass in Latin than in the vernacular, third, there was total silence during the Consecration, and fourth, there was no fundraising like we normally do after Post-Communion prayers in the NO and I was surprised when the priest sang the *"Ite, Missa est"* just after Communion, all of which are things I hated seeing in the NO and they never happened in the Mass and so after the Mass, I knew deep in my heart that I had found a treasure and I must sell all I had to possess it.

The next Sunday, June 13th, was the Feast of St. Anthony of Padua. After the Mass, there was a Rosary Procession in honor of the Apparition of Our Lady of Fatima which pleased me so much. I wouldn't make it for the next two Sundays to Mass due to financial constraints (or so as I like to tell myself) but when I came back, it was a return never to go back to where I came from. Little by little, tradition began to appeal to me and my admiration for it grew exponentially. For a while, I juggled between coming to Mass on Sundays and going to the NO in school during weekdays where I took the Mass readings but after some time, I left the Lectors and joined the Altar Servers in my new Parish and in January of 2022, I served my first Mass. I know I made a few mistakes here and there but believe me when I tell you that it was a wonderful experience, more than I can ever describe.

Before I move to the next section, I must say that I am not endorsing social media. I have been tempted to tell myself before that without it, I probably would not have seen the Mass, in order to convince myself that social media is something good in itself but that's not true. Social media is evil, fly from it! My own case is an example of how the good Lord can create good even from evil, or at least, that's how I see it now.

It has now been three years since I started assisting at the TLM and for all I can say, there has not been anything like these last three years, nothing comes even close. These years have by far been the best years of my life and the best part of it is that each successive year is always better than the one preceding it. Now there are lots of benefits to talk about which assisting at the TLM has afforded me, each as important as the other but for want of space, I will actually limit my writing to a selected few.

The first thing I realized when I started assisting at the TLM was my utter ignorance of the Catholic Faith; don't get me wrong, I actually knew my catechism by heart but I never knew what most of those words meant nor had I a deeper understanding of them but then when I started coming to the TLM and listening to sermons and attending catechism classes afterwards and reading good books, everything changed and now I know sufficiently enough to defend my Faith whenever it is attacked. I think the obligation to know the Faith is stressed far more in the TLM than in the NO and every action of the priest, every activity in the Parish is designed to inculcate the Catholic Faith to parishioners. I also learnt for the first time that was something very beautiful called the Catholic culture which transcends every other culture. One would not readily grasp what this means, especially in this part of the globe except what one considers the product of this great culture in Europe. The best part of this education was that it was a practical, not just intellectual, I mean I saw it in application to things both big like having a Catholic family and small like saying Grace before and after meals.

The second thing that needs to be mentioned is the rapid growth in my spiritual life. Day after day, Mass after Mass, the injunction to be perfect as Christ was resounded and vehemently emphasized. The love God bears to us and the love we must bear to him was the more insisted. Little by little, I started realizing that I had been merely existing, how I must live for God alone and how I must do every action for His pleasure. The need to do penance and offer up our daily mortification to God in expiation for our sins, to pray for the souls in Purgatory, to be devoted to Our Lady, the Angels and the Saints was the constant subject of every day's sermon. Praying the Rosary daily, daily mental prayer and spiritual reading was encouraged. I had been a voracious reader and so switching to reading Catholic books was not that hard for me and now I have read more than 20 books and have about 15 in my personal collection with hope of getting more. All these made me realize that I have a soul to save which made a great impression on my spiritual life and now as St. Louis de Montfort wrote in his *True Devotion to Mary*, "we make more progress in just a few days of submitting to Mary than in many years on our own," I can equally say that I have made much more spiritual progress in these three years assisting at the TLM than in my years in the NO combined.

The next benefit that comes to mind is the beauty and joy I experience every Sunday serving in the Sanctuary. On these days, I have the privilege of literally being close to God. This joy is something only one who has served at Mass can describe, if he actually can. Learning the Mass responses was not a big deal because I have this love for the Latin like I pointed out earlier so much that I am currently learning the language from a book my Parish Priest lent me and I hope to be fluent someday. The most fascinating thing about serving Mass is that it stresses more the unity of the Church. Moving to another geographical area would not hinder me from serving Mass insofar as there is the TLM, the responses and movements are the same. I found solace in the fact that even if I move to Europe, to a Church I haven't been to before, I would kneel at the foot of the Altar beside a priest and I will respond "Ad Deum qui laetificat juventutem meam" when he says "Introibo ad Altare Dei." This thought fills me with great consolation. There are still more beautiful things to talk about but for want of time and space, I will stop here.

Talking about what the TLM means to me, the first thing that really came to my mind when I thought about it was that if there was just one thing that is right in this world, if anything is true, good and beautiful, it would be the Traditional Latin Mass, but then the irony that it doubles as the most persecuted thing in the world stresses further how decayed our world is. But even though the Mass is persecuted, I cannot imagine a life or future without it. I cannot imagine the future of my children, if God permits me any, without it. This is how much the Mass means to me.

Again, the TLM has been the source of my faith. Every day, in that piercing silence, the TLM has worked laboriously in the task of building my faith helping me love God more, not just with the catechisms but in every action of the priest–the genuflections, the signs of the Cross, the bows, the reverence, the silence — all of which reminds me, louder than any word that Jesus Christ is truly present in the Blessed Sacrament and so the Mass is truly important to me because it has been the source of all my little effort to love God and remain very close to Him.

The Mass has been the epicentre of true friendship. After the Mass on Sundays is a great time for hanging out with people of like minds, people I cannot do without. This friendship is integral in the community simply because people look out for other people and so these relationships are also very important to me, and they would not have been brought about if there was no TLM.

The Latin Mass means so much to me than I have already described, so much so that if you took away the Mass, I sincerely doubt that I would save my soul.

29. A SERVER'S EXPERIENCE OF THE TRADITIONAL MASS
Joseph, Age 16. New Hampshire

I HAD AN INTERESTING INTRODUCTION TO THE Latin Mass. My mom moved up to New Hampshire from Dallas, Texas, twenty-eight years ago. While in Texas, she had access to the Latin Mass, provided by the Priestly Fraternity of St. Peter (FSSP). Once she moved up to New England, however, that privilege was no longer available. For twenty years, she prayed that the FSSP would establish one of their apostolates close by. In 2016, it was announced by the Diocese of Manchester that a church in Nashua, NH, would be reopening and staffed by the FSSP to provide the Traditional Latin Mass and sacraments to the Diocese of Manchester. My mother was thrilled. This was the answer to twenty long years of prayer. She explained to us that it would be different from what we were used to and that we probably wouldn't know what was going on at first, but that didn't matter. All we needed to do was watch the priest and listen. The priest would be praying to God, not talking to us.

The church, St. Stanislaus, was a ten-minute drive from our house. Not only were we able to attend Sunday Mass at a Latin Mass, but we were also able to go to weekday Mass. My dad was a little hesitant about going, as he had some trust issues with the Church. However, my mom told him to go to Mass for four weeks in a row without flip-flopping back and forth to the Novus Ordo. By the fifth week, he would have a better understanding of what was going on. He would also most likely grow closer to the Latin Mass. By the end of the first week, he was hooked. He never looked back.

We then left our Novus Ordo parish. We had a conundrum, however. My brother and I had been serving Mass on Wednesday mornings there. We decided we would continue to do that for the foreseeable future, as we had made a commitment. That ended up lasting three years.

Meanwhile, I got involved in St. Stanislaus' serving program. Most of the boys who were the first servers at St. Stanislaus had volunteered from other parishes. They eventually switched churches and attended St. Stan's full time. However, there was still a server shortage. Also, the boys couldn't come and serve daily Mass, as they were in school.

I, however, was able to do that. I started to learn how to serve Low Mass. I had learned the basics of the rubrics but was still working on my responses. One day, ten minutes before Mass, I went to confession. When I exited the confessional, I realized that the altar was not set up or ready for Mass. I walked back into the confessional and asked Father if he would like me to set up the altar and serve for him. He said yes. I promptly put on a cassock and surplice and prepared the altar for Mass. For the most part, I served fine. I needed a few pointers here and there, but otherwise, I had the actions nailed down. The responses, on the other hand, were a different story. I hadn't memorized any of my responses yet. How was I to serve Mass if I couldn't respond to the priest? A solution was found. One of the parishioners in the front row recited the responses for me, and I performed the actions. This went on for a little while longer until I memorized my responses. For the first year or so, only one server would be scheduled per Mass. If a second server was in the church for Mass, he could volunteer to serve as well. For the first few months, other men would attempt to serve with me. Father told them that I could manage just fine on my own. This gave me a great boost of confidence. Eventually, I started serving with other boys more and more.

Our altar serving group is called the Knights of the Altar. We have a board of officers who are in charge of the boys. There are ranks and other positions. In the beginning, I was just one of the boys who attended the meetings and learned. However, the group took a break during COVID. When we resumed meetings, I was elected head of the group, even though I was only 12 years old. This put a great deal of responsibility on me. But that helped me. Now, I am no longer in charge, but in the time that I was the Supreme Grand Knight, I learned a lot about leading, as well as other virtues.

One highly noticeable difference between the Latin Mass and the Novus Ordo is the language. A lot of people would say that the N. O. is superior in this respect, as it uses the vernacular, which can be understood by all who live in that area. However, it is truly the Latin Mass that is better in this category. Latin lends an air of mystery, which is appropriate for celebrating the Holy Sacrifice of the Mass. Latin is a universal language. It is not the primary language of any country and is a dead language. For this reason, it does not change; the meanings of the words are fixed. Thus, the Church utilizes it because a Catholic can go anywhere in the world and attend the exact same mass as back home. He still has the exact same understanding of the prayers as if he's in his customary pew back in his local parish. The introduction and spread of the Novus Ordo have taken away that availability for Catholics. One will be lucky if he can find a missal that translates a foreign Mass into his vernacular.

Another beauty of the Tridentine Mass is that the form does not change. All of the actions are the same around the world. A server could serve a Latin Mass in Virginia, USA, and one in Italy, without worrying about the local customs. A Novus Ordo server would probably experience some difficulty trying to do the same thing. Apart from the language difficulty, the priest in Virginia would probably have different customs than the priest in Italy. I myself have had a similar experience. Obviously, I've served at St. Stanislaus. I've also served at my summer camp. Both Masses were Latin. There was no difference. I served them both with perfect ease. I've also served the Novus Ordo in a few different churches. It was different in each parish. I had to ask the pastor what his personal preferences were before each Mass.

There is also a supreme sense of reverence in the Tridentine Mass, as opposed to the Novus Ordo. There are a few reasons for this. One is that the priest faces towards the altar, away from the congregation. When the priest is facing the people and making eye contact with them, it is more tempting to turn the Mass into a form of entertainment. The priest is more likely to use jokes in his sermon and not be as serious during the Mass. The Tridentine priest, however, does not have these temptations. He faces away from the people, making the Mass solely about God. Another difference is the music. Music used in the N. O. is often targeted at the congregation singing along and making them feel as though they are participating. Music in the Latin Mass is entirely in Latin, making it slightly more difficult for the congregation to insert themselves in the participation. There is a difference between participation in the N. O. compared to the Latin. In the Novus Ordo, participation consists of saying the responses and singing along. In the Latin Mass, participation means being at Mass and praying internally with the priest. In the Tridentine Mass, the servers say the responses and the choir sings. The combination of all these factors makes the Latin Mass more reverent, more focused on God.

The Latin Mass has left an impact on me for many reasons. Even though I didn't exactly understand what was going on the first time I attended that Rite, I could tell something was different. And I liked that. As the years have passed, I've learned more and more about this form of the Mass. Getting to serve it has helped me learn about it more than anything. Being able to be that close to the Holy Sacrifice of the Mass has had a great impact on me. Being able to be more exposed to the Latin language through the Mass has not only been enriching but has helped me in my studies. The reverence has made me appreciate this form of the Mass more than anything else. Being able to go to different parishes and see the difference in the way they handle the reverence of the Mass has been truly enlightening. The Latin Mass has also helped me grow spiritually, revealing things about myself that I didn't even know about. It has also helped me navigate difficult things.

We are now approaching eight years since our parish opened, which means I have been attending the Traditional Latin Mass for half of my life now. Even though I do occasionally attend a Novus Ordo Mass, I am most at home with the Latin and would seek it out wherever I go. I am grateful that I have been introduced to this Rite and am keenly aware of how blessed I am to have a TLM parish with daily Mass and confessions only ten minutes from my home.

30. "WHY DID THEY EVER CHANGE IT?"
Olisa, Age 20, Nigeria

MY WRISTWATCH LET OUT A SHARP BEEP from the table to indicate the top of the hour. It was 3 pm, my cue to start getting ready for Mass. And it wasn't for the first time that Sunday. It was another odd week Sunday in the month and so there would be Mass at the chapel – the Latin Mass. Such had been my routine for some time now. I attended Masses at our usual parish in the morning and when the occasion presented, I went to the SSPX chapel which had Mass once every two weeks at 4 pm. It was 2022; tertiary institutions were on strike, and we were home for 8 months.

I first came across the Traditional Latin Mass (TLM) while in school. Someone had mentioned it to me colloquially as the "back altar Mass" referring to the fact that the priest has his back to the congregation, and how there was a group of students who go there every Sunday. The FSSP parish is the only one in our area and is coincidentally located about 40km away from the Federal University of Technology, Owerri. Out of curiosity, I decided to attend on a particular Sunday. It was very different to anything I'd ever seen before, and I was quite struck by it. I had lots of questions afterwards, the chief of them being "Why did they ever change it?"

However, I didn't think much of it afterwards. My attendance at the TLM was infrequent after this. I do believe that those occasional Sundays when I did go were graces which eventually got me to this point. I was still curious and so, I began to read: the history of the church, the second Vatican Council, the advent of modernism, the "excommunications" and so on. More importantly, I found the Church's tradition in all its splendour. I came across things about the faith that I had never heard or even come across and my interest was further piqued.

Sometimes, one is wont to acquire knowledge simply for the sake of it and maybe this was the case. But eventually, I began to see the Mass in a different light. All I had come to know made the Novus Ordo Mass make less and less sense. Surely, there was something much more to this than a difference in language and orientation between the two masses. I started to feel unsatisfied at my normal parish Mass. It was this yearning that led to my subsequent search for the TLM at home and a deeper delve into traditional Catholicism.

My story would be incomplete if I did not mention my consecration to Our Lady. We returned to school and within the next year, I joined the 33-day preparatory class for total consecration to Jesus through Mary. This is organized by the Confraternity of Mary, Queen of all Hearts. It was Our Lady who showed me this more excellent way and helped me to truly find the Mass. I gained a lot more conviction and as time has gone by. I now attend the TLM regularly.

For one, the Mass embodies the True, the Good and the Beautiful. It's so clear to see the end to which everything is directed. In the rubrics, prayers, and movements, in the order and setting, in the beautiful chants and sacred music, in the deafening silence which took some getting used to, I saw it. Not immediately, but I did. By making this highest form of worship a central part of our lives, it trickles down into every other thing we do. Because what else are we on earth for if not to be united to God, who is Truth, Goodness, and Beauty?

I remember the Easter vigil Mass of my first TLM Triduum. I felt robbed. It is no wonder the Church calls it the height of its liturgy. How could such a precious and beautiful thing have been taken away from us? It was akin to lighting a candle and putting it under a bushel! I could have relived it a million times over. And so, it was at every other Mass. It was the mystery of it all that made it appealing and gave it the sense of something sacred, something fitting for the worship of God. I realize what a tremendous grace it is to have found this and I am grateful to God for it.

Moreover, a major highlight of what the TLM has meant to me is the difference in spirituality. Being at the TLM has made me understand what it means to live a truly Catholic life. Prior to this, I was very indifferent about a lot of things which concerned my spiritual life. I look back at those times and I am grateful for now. Although (while I hope to be) I do not claim to be a saint yet, I now realize how important it is to work for the salvation of my soul, such that everything I do should be for this one necessary thing. Even without hearing a sermon, attending a conference, coming for catechism, or going on a retreat, simply being at Mass makes you realize what is truly important, for everything has God at its centre.

A beautiful thing was that I actually began to pray. Not in the way I had come to know all my life — with the absence of attention and devotion and centred on self. I saw it for what it was really meant to be: a lifting of our minds and hearts to God, just like the way the saints did. It became more regular and has come to hold a prominent place in my state of life. The daily rosary, mental prayer, and other wonderful devotions which I picked up have been truly wonderful and aided me in my spiritual journey.

I began to read more spiritual books and learn more about the saints and the Catholic faith in general. I came across things that inspired me to grow in virtue, increased my zeal and made me want to love God more. It is like a treasure trove which one stumbles upon, not filled with the perishable things of this world but with incredible objects that give you a glimpse of eternity. I would liken it to the treasure which our Lord speaks of, hidden in a field. "Which a man having found, hid it, and for joy thereof goeth, and selleth all that he hath, and buyeth that field".

A few weeks back, in publishing our graduating class yearbook, we were all asked to fill out a section for "most memorable moment." I gave it some thought and put down "finding the Mass." I cannot say exactly when or even how it happened, but it did and for that, I am thankful.

31. TRANSFORMED BY TRADITION: A JEWISH CONVERT'S JOURNEY
Kai, Age 19, New York

ONE CAN IMAGINE WHAT COMES WITH BEING raised Jewish in New York: I attended a Jewish Private School for some years, then a Hebrew after-school program, and had a Bar-Mitzvah, but never believed in much. My family is quite secular so while we would celebrate most of the annual Jewish holidays, we would rarely pray together and never attended Saturday morning services.

Religion and belief in God had always been something I had taken for granted, so it became a strong interest for me to discover the truth. My closest friend in high school was a stringent atheist and through conversations with him, I had my intellectual pursuits challenged and tested. At the time I had a strange fascination with studying Christianity. Growing up Jewish, this was not only a topic that wasn't discussed, but it was also never considered interesting enough to look into. I became very interested in Christianity's history, its different sects and groups, and its diversity of theological positions, histories, and practices. I found myself squared with the central truth claim of Christianity: Did Jesus of Nazareth rise from the dead? We of course profess that this is an actual historical event that took place 2,000 years ago, and to be a Christian one must believe it too. On the surface, this is quite striking and frankly absurd. How could someone come to believe that, let alone prove it historically? However, I slowly realized that there was better evidence than most people assume, and after much research and self-reflection, I came to believe it as well. Through this process, I similarly came to the same understanding of the Catholic Faith as the true and only Christian Church of all ages.

After making this leap intellectually, I knew I had to put it into practice in some way. As a result, on Sunday, May 9th, 2021, I attended Mass for the first time at the Church of St. Vincent Ferrer in Manhattan which is a gorgeous and massive Dominican-run Church in New York City. For someone who had never been to any Christian service before and had no expectations or preconceived notions, I thoroughly enjoyed it. Incense was used, the Creed was sung with

English plainchant, and the breathtaking art and architecture certainly elevated my spirits.

During this time of listening to Catholic Answers and learning as much as I could about the faith I started hearing things about the Latin Mass, how the Mass used to be, and whatnot; I simply made the assumption—as most Catholics do—that the only difference to the service before they changed things and after was that they translated it and the priest now faces the other way. It was under this impression that I attended my first Traditional Mass at the Shrine and Parish Church of the Holy Innocents in midtown Manhattan. It was only by spontaneous conversation that someone invited me after I mentioned my curiosity. I hadn't known there was a Latin Mass in New York City and so was eager for the opportunity to attend.

The Sunday was the 16th after Pentecost on September 12th of the same year, the small and intimate Church was buzzing with souls on fire and silent contemplation, as it always is, and I sat back with few expectations and much excitement.

There is a tendency that attendees of the Latin Mass have which makes us often assume that as soon as we take someone, they are going to instantly understand why so many people like this, why it's so serious, and perhaps even that they'll ask to convert on the spot or weeping of joy. Although this is possible, it is usually not what happens, and it isn't what happened to me. I did enjoy the Latin Mass the first time I went; the music was unfamiliar yet prayerful and the silence was powerful, but I didn't understand everything. It took the continual outpouring of love that the sacred liturgy gives us to win my heart.

Upon attending for several months, I fell in love. Dare I say as intimately as a man loves his wife, I was head over heels for the Traditional Liturgy. For approximately a year I exclusively attended the Latin Mass. I always sought it out despite longer travel times. I studied the texts and the rubrics extensively, falling in love with every prayer, especially in its fitting place in the *Lingua Sacra*. I admired the liturgical cycle of readings, orations, and antiphons, the beauty of traditional vestments, and the fittingness of the ceremony in which we entered. I began a self-study of Gregorian Chant and sang the great corpus of music weekly at Mass, and daily in my free time. I even closely analyzed and spectated every movement of the priest at the altar. I was enthralled by the ravishing beauty of Traditional Catholic worship.

It took another year until my reception into the Church. Truthfully this was one of the hardest things I have had to endure. For two years I was outside the church waiting to be let in, yet I had no countdown. I yearned to receive the Eucharist; every time I had been to Mass before, every Sunday, every feast day, every time I was with my friends, I always stood back as everyone else received. All I wanted was to receive Our Lord, and to finally be a Catholic.

In the spring of my first year of college, I was finally received into the Church. Thanks to much of God's grace and providence I received Baptism and Confirmation in the traditional rite at the Easter Vigil in 2023. This was also my first time attending the rites of Holy Week as well, I was more than excited. The rite of the Easter Vigil could only be described as glorious; I was so moved by the twelve readings, the vestments being changed from violet to gold, the beautiful music, and of course the Baptismal rite. It was only three days after that when I first served Low Mass and I very quickly began to take any opportunity to serve at the Altar and learn more about the sacred Liturgy.

Because of my background, I have been increasingly edified by the Mass in how it presents itself in a like manner to the Holy Temple in Jerusalem. From the incense, chant, vestments, and the use of a sacred tongue, the trifold understanding of the sacrifice, to the awe-inspiring use of the Psalms in the old missal, something struck me deeply about Christian worship that I can almost not explain. Our Lord says that He is the fulfillment of the Law and that His risen body is the temple restored; because of this, we should be able to see a continuity. There are even minuscule details of the liturgy which mirror the temple worship. One example of this is found during the Eucharistic Prayer at the specific prayer known as the Hanc Igitur. At this point of the Mass, the priest elevates his hands over the offering as he makes reference to the sacrifice he is about to consecrate. This was the same action that the Levites would make in the Temple over the animal before it was to be slain.

One other example is found, at least in the Roman Rite, after the priest offers bread and wine, he makes the sign of the cross with each one before placing them down. We know from the Jewish oral traditions that the Levites in the temple would do the same thing, of course without the understanding of the symbol of the cross. The symbolism is rather that after the victim is offered, the priest would move it in the direction of the four points of the compass to symbolize that the God it was being offered to is the Lord over all the earth.

    The glory of the sacred liturgy is unmatched and unparalleled on this side of eternity, and it has become the joy of my life to understand its sacrality, theology, deep symbolism, and mystery. I have found the Latin Mass to be so awe inspiring, so captivating, so precise, so divine yet human, complex yet simple, that it entices my very soul to move up to God. When at Mass I often imagine, as I say along with the Priest the line from Psalm 42, "Introibo ad altare Dei" "I will go unto the Altar of God," that I am in the Temple of Solomon hearing the Levites say those same exact words.

32. NO LONGER A LOST SHEEP
Abigail, Age 20, North Dakota

SANCTUS, SANCTUS, SANCTUS.
I imagine those words sung by the angels as they are spoken ring signal that we are about to enter the Canon of the Mass, where Jesus will soon be presented in an unbloody manner in the most holy and perfect Blessed Sacrament. I watch and wait in longing as the priest prepares to consecrate Him Who Is with specific gestures handed down through a 2,000-year-old liturgy. I stare at the tabernacle in front of the priest, knowing that it houses my Creator, my Redeemer, and my Judge. And then I watch closely for the moment when He humbles Himself to be my propitiation, my salvation, and my hope. When the priest lifts the Host before the congregation and repeats *"Dómine, non sum dignus..."* (Lord, I am not worthy...) I see His unrecognizable, tortured body staring down into my soul as I press my forehead onto the wood of the cross under His feet, where streams of blood that would rather be forgotten somehow stream over my insignificant forehead.

This is a snippet of the effect the Traditional Latin Mass has had on my faith and ultimately on my soul. It has completely transformed my life. Let me explain.

I was born into the Catholic Church, and while I did not receive a deep catechesis, my family always made it a point to go to Mass every Sunday. However, there was always something in me that desired more, to know Him better. Around fifth grade, I started to question my faith quite seriously, especially regarding confession and different salvific interpretations of the Bible. I hated confession, Church teaching sounded impossible to follow, and I just wasn't really sure the Catholic Faith was the True Faith. I agonized over this throughout middle school, and there were many sleepless nights where I felt God would never show me whether I needed to be Protestant or Catholic. How then, could I be saved? I didn't really know what I was searching for, and that was probably the most frustrating part. I went through spurts of energy, trying to find anything, really, but ended up more discouraged than before; I did not have the support to endure the attacks that I was faced with when I attempted to make spiritual progress.

I had no idea where to turn. I knew that Protestantism did not have much for me (I had studied conservative and liberal Protestant theology for some time), but I also would not accept the teachings of the Church. I became incredibly stagnant. Even though I made the decision to take a "break" from religion, I knew I could not stay in that place. I realized I needed to be prepared for college before I fell to the snare of poor influence and spiritual death. I started to ask Jesus if he could send me a friend to show me the *whole* Truth, to prepare me for the endurance of university life.

Not long after, I met a Catholic co-worker who knew her faith very well. I asked her many questions, even though I was still not completely convinced. Eventually, she invited me to a Latin Mass she attended a couple of times. Even though I visited blindly, I could see that there was something deeply reverent and self-sacrificial in its nature that I had never witnessed prior. This Mass was nearly unrecognizable to me as a Catholic! A few months later, I had been intellectually convinced of Catholicism and decided to give myself completely to Christ by making a good confession, with the resolution of being wholly Catholic and never looking back. It was at this point (the beginning of my senior year of high school) in which I went to the Latin Mass and traditional confession consistently. It was also at this point when the spiritual attacks I had suffered before came back with a deep vengeance.

Living in mortal sin was like being chained to the bottom of the ocean while slowly drowning, and I didn't even realize it. After I made my good confession, the chains were cut, but I still had to struggle to swim to the top. Each day was a long and difficult battle. However, the greatest sufferings also come with the greatest graces, which certainly flowed through the Latin Mass. Each week I became more immersed in the *ad orientem* worship, modest dress and veiling of women, traditional confession, Catholic family life, and the rich structure of the Traditional Latin Mass.

Gradually, the principle of *lex orandi, lex credendi, lex vivendi* (the law of what is prayed [is] what is believed [is] the law of what is lived) became most apparent in my life when going to the Latin Mass. As I learned to pray in the Mass, and especially after learning to follow along in a 1962 Missal, I started to learn about the theology and significance of the Mass deeper and deeper. The prayers established and perfected over the course of 2,000 years are key to the understanding of The Faith; as a result, the content of the Mass has been very important in the catechesis of my mind and heart. "Let not the partaking of Thy Body, O Lord Jesus Christ, which I, all unworthy, presume to receive, turn to my judgment and condemnation; but through Thy loving kindness may it be to me a safeguard and remedy for soul and body..." is just one example of words I have never known in a liturgy prior to attending the Latin Mass. Knowing these words remind me how gravely important it is to be in the State of Grace, and the dependency us poor souls have on Him in the Blessed Sacrament in order to stay in it. How often I have neglected Our Lord when I have received Him! In my stagnancy I had mentioned earlier, I had certainly received Our Lord carelessly and unworthily. How much more would I continue to live tepidly, which is the ultimate drug of thinking everything is fine? This prayer has thus informed my belief in the Eucharist, which affects my prayer during Mass, and thus pushes me to live in a way which is conducive to receiving Jesus every day. All of the other components contained within the Latin Mass also continue to permeate the way I believe and thus inform the way I live, which are drastically different now that I am attending the Latin Mass.

I also noticed that I pray much better. I have learned that the environment presented in the TLM such as silence, Gregorian Chant, and *ad orientem* lift the heart to God in a way that nothing else does. These aspects of the Mass give me space to practice giving myself more and more to Jesus. Without this space, I find myself in a sort of cognitive dissonance in which my attempts to pray are reflected back by an invisible wall of noise which hinders my ability to focus on preparing my soul for Holy Communion. When the graces I receive during the Mass are dependent upon my disposition, how much more should I seek a liturgy which is most conducive to taking the focus off myself and onto Christ, who is deserving of all that I have and am? I have realized that the structure and environment built into the Latin Mass are there to support and allow this lowly species to give due reverence to that which God deserves.

In addition, I have observed that Jesus in the Blessed Sacrament is treated with a drastic difference in the Latin Mass in comparison to the average Novus Ordo Mass. The TLM was the first time I had received Jesus kneeling, on the tongue, and has changed my perspective on the seriousness of the Person I am about to receive. A couple of months into going to the Latin Mass, I went back to my parent's Novus Ordo Mass to fulfill a Holy Day of Obligation. It was strange, because my mindset was completely different; it was almost as if a switch had flipped in the way I treated the Holy Eucharist. Consequently, I showed up to Mass in jeans and a t-shirt instead of a modest dress, walked up to an Extraordinary Eucharistic Minister instead of the priest for Holy Communion, and presented my hands instead of my tongue to receive Jesus. Worst of all, when I went to place the Host on my tongue, it slipped from my palms and onto the floor. The EMHC then proceeded to pick it up and handed me another one like nothing had happened. I nearly fainted. How many particles of Our Lord were left on the ground that day? How many more particles of the Sacred Heart are trampled each day He is not received with a paten under the tongue from consecrated hands? My heart breaks into pieces each time I witness it. Where are the reparations?

When I had my conversion back to the Faith, I had no idea how much it would require of me. The attacks I suffered continued aggressively through my senior year of high school, and I certainly would have crumbled had I lacked this ancient liturgy to sustain me. As a result, this beautiful Mass is more than my preference, but a consistent foundation in my spiritual life which I completely depend on to grow in Christ and stay in the State of Grace. By the end of the summer after my senior year, I had the strength to manage my spiritual battles, an understanding of my basic catechesis, was given a 1962 Missal, and had my very own veil. God had truly worked in my life to prepare me for college. I was no longer one of His lost sheep.

Now, I am 20 years old and have continued to grow in The Faith. Through the Traditional Latin Mass and the guidance of traditional priests, I have been led deeper into the rich treasures of the Church and in virtue. I have grown to love Our Lady in the Rosary, the writings of Church fathers, meditation, plenary indulgences, charity towards the Holy Souls of Purgatory, and the profound value of sacrifice in conjunction with prayer, just to name a few. Above all, I am learning how to love the Sacred Heart and Immaculate Heart of Mary by offering myself wholly and completely to repair the horrible outrages committed against them. Had I not been led to this Mass, I would not know Christ and Sacred Tradition as I do today, and I would have missed celebrating the inheritance which sustained nearly all of the saints, and which now sustains my soul.

The Latin Mass has truly been my *lex orandi, lex credendi, lex vivendi*, and completely transformed the way I believe, pray, dress, speak, work, and, ultimately, live. I did not know it was possible to know Jesus like this! This is what I have been longing for my entire life! Let us cry *Sanctus, Sanctus, Sanctus* with the angels as the priest elevates our Perfect Savior in union with the martyrs and saints. I am willing to die for this Mass. This is the Mass of the Ages. This is the Traditional Latin Mass.

33. THE TRADITIONAL MASS IS A "REALITY CHECK"
Marta, Age 16, Philippines

WHAT MAKES SOMETHING APPEALING? HOW interesting, significant, or powerful must something be for you to continually choose it? When my parents slowly eased my siblings and I to attending slightly longer, "different," further-from-home Latin Masses, I went as an obligated 8-year-old.

My family's usual Sunday was simple: get up at 8AM–a treat when compared to our 6AM school day wake up–stuff our faces with Dad's pancakes, get changed by Mom, and jump in the van just in time for my elder brother and I to join the choir. The weekly almost-hour went by quickly as I sang Church songs practiced the day before and overlooked pews filled with familiar faces.

Then, every so often, my parents would drive us to a Traditional Latin Mass in a small chapel half an hour away. Internally, I disliked the change. 8AM mornings became 7:30, our time in the car doubled, and I was facing micro changes I wasn't particularly excited to tell my friends about.

Van rides would be loud and chatty; the new chapel was conversely peaceful and solemn, elderly *lolos*, *lolas* and the occasional young family (as we were) reciting silent rosaries and prayers before Mass. It was remarkably reverent in a way that I couldn't understand then. I didn't anticipate that as we became regular attendees, we'd become accustomed to this more traditional "norm". Through these liturgies, I learned to be more intentional about the TLM. My siblings and I would read off the missals, uber-conscious of which page our parents were on; take Communion while kneeling in our more formal outfits, us girls in veils. These small differences were a basis for many questions asked to Mom and Dad, prompting conversations to better understand the Latin ceremony.

After a while, this first small chapel closed. For a time, my family would go to different churches, and travel times evolved to forty minutes, twenty minutes, an hour. I realized that among every single Church, chapel, home – there were two constants: the Latin Mass, and a collective of participants. In between the pews and chairs, crammed in the back-most rows or involuntarily in the choir loft;

sometimes without any air conditioning or directly under the sun. Individuals, young families, elderly couples who shared, if not the devotion, an interest in the TLM. It was being in a room with strangers who I knew would understand very nuanced, spiritual thoughts and dilemmas. This was interesting company, of ladies singing in the choir, brothers and dads helping as altar servers, and attendees fanning their seatmates when the aircon didn't reach either.

It's beautiful to think of how these figures I've met through the TLM have integrated into my personal life. For the last 3 years, my house has hosted the same priest and ladies from Church, one of them now my godmother, for my dad's birthday dinner. Circles coalesce, and I see familiar faces in societies for devotions, neighborhood committees, and personal friendships. Time spent with these people is always time spent meaningfully, and it is extremely reassuring to have connections who share my values.

This exact community is living social proof of individuals who wake up before daybreak, travel much longer than half an hour, and particularly seek Christ in the Latin Mass. They desire the wholeness specifically found in this traditional liturgy.

The Traditional Latin Mass is not new. It is an antique ceremony prayed by our ancestors as a holier, more devout form of worship. I believe that Faith was practiced differently then – it oversaw people's actions, the way they dressed, and the way they talked. They practiced virtues often and were able to openly express their love for God. Despite modernism and the many temptations of the present, the TLM acts as a "reality check" due to its wholeness and devoutness. By attending these Masses every Sunday, I am reminded of the virtues and character that I must live out every day. I am encouraged to be patient in difficult times, humble as I learn and grow, and understanding when interacting with others.

Perhaps the most significant realization I've had through the traditional liturgy was during the pandemic. As the world shut down, days were indistinguishable and my family would go from regular COVID-19 activities (think: puzzles, baking bread, and watching MasterClass) to dressing up, getting our veils and missals, and praying the Latin Mass in our living room. This nimble switch, as well as popping-up videos on Instagram of praying Christians and Catholics, slowly introduced me to informal, conversational prayers. Rather than solely before meals, before bed, and at Church, I began to understand that pausing my task in the middle of the day to talk to God, or conversing with Him as I worked, was natural. It was almost too simple: live Christ-centered every day, converse with your Father about the mundane! It would recenter my thinking and put a smile on my face for the rest of the day.

When my family began attending the Latin Mass, I went because 8-year-olds don't really have a choice. Now a fully conscious and critical teenager, it would be reasonable to call my parents, carpool with a friend, and attend a novus ordo.

I wholeheartedly believe that the beauty of the Traditional Latin Mass is in the reverence and tradition it instills in attendees of all ages and from all walks of life. It is a cornerstone for Christ-centered relationships and communities, and a foundation for deeper personal faith. Even with the freedom to choose, the Latin Mass remains my preference. The experiences and lessons I acquire on this journey equip and empower me to better serve and love both God and neighbor in my day-to-day life.

34. GOD, WHO GIVETH JOY TO MY YOUTH
Maja, Age 19, Virginia

THE BELL RINGS. I STAND IN THE BACK OF THE crowded church and await the murmur of the priest above the familiar echoes of the creaking pews and the sound of dress shoes on the old marble floor. "In nòmine Patris... Introíbo ad altáre Dei." Although I have heard it more than once a week for six years now and could probably say the response forwards and backwards, my heart still leaps with eternally fresh gratitude as I pray inaudibly along with the faint voice of the altar servers "Ad Deum qui laetíficat juventútem meam."

This is the story of how the Holy Spirit showed me my identity in the Faith and in the Church by introducing me to the home I now have in the Traditional Latin Mass. A person's sense of identity is formed primarily–at least ideally–in the home, and my home was always temperamentally traditional. When my parents moved us to Germany in 2015 and my father began working for the U. S. Department of Defense's European Command, we were about as traditionally Catholic as we thought possible. My mother had long since left a successful career to be a stay-at-home homeschooling mother of five children. I had convinced my mother and sister to start wearing chapel veils, all of us (except for the baby) were learning Latin, and a few of us were even zealous, if inexperienced, pupils of Gregorian chant. None of these things were unusual in the parish we had just left, where faithful Dominican priests celebrated a beautiful Novus Ordo and hosted a weekly homeschool co-op. This certainly contributed to our surprise upon discovering the local Mass options in Germany.

Relying on the universality of Catholicism and hoping for their children to make friends with all the Catholic children in the village, my parents invested much energy into integrating our family into our local German parish. The liturgy, however, was unrecognizable. Dramatized sermons theatrically presented through acting teams, "priestesses" in albs with scarves as stoles, liturgical dance, and the surprise of our new German acquaintances that we were regularly there–even when no one in our family was receiving a Sacrament that day–were increasingly difficult to excuse. Our church's Catholic summer camp refused to bring the campers to Sunday Mass, so my parents drove 1-2 hours to take us 10 minutes away to a local Mass, after which we would return to the camp. The local Christian girls' club was pressuring me into dressing tastelessly and the youth group where volunteers taught us drinking games with apple juice. Slowly these influences contributed to a growing insecurity about my Catholic faith. After all, if only my parents believed in modesty, temperance, and other higher virtues, was it really possible that everyone else I knew was entirely wrong?

My parents decided to end their foray into the German church by attending Mass on the military base in what was essentially a bright conference room which Catholic military families shared with those of various other faiths, including Muslims and even Pagans. At the end of each Mass, altar servers hid the tabernacle and the Stations of the Cross, and removed the crucifix along with statues of Mary, St. Joseph, and St. Michael. The reverence at Mass on base depended largely on the military chaplain or local contract priest who happened to be there that day. One never knew whether one was about to hear a beautifully catechetical sermon delivered by a Nigerian priest who had undergone physical persecution in his native country for wearing a Roman collar or receive the Holy Eucharist on Christmas Eve to the strains of Jingle Bells karaoke played from a MacBook placed on the altar (both true stories).

None of this narrative is meant to disparage the people in those communities, all of whom were seeking God. Many were merely misguided by poor leadership and the gradual but steady lukewarm influence of secular society. Many American families felt they had no choice, being stationed abroad without the ability to speak the local vernacular. We began to experience spiritual starvation for the beauty and orthodoxy we remembered from some of our parishes in the United States. My parents watched this with growing concern until one summer, when I was in middle school, a family from our old co-op visited us in Germany. They listened sympathetically to our complaints and showed almost saintly patience, considering our long lack of interest in their choice to attend the Traditional Latin Mass, a form of the liturgy that we had never even experienced.

Surely, they told us, the traditional orders would offer summer camps with Sunday Mass. Upon this prompting, my mother called one of them to ask if the camp provided transportation for Holy Mass on Sunday. The thoroughly flummoxed priest (who has since become a wonderful friend of ours) asked my mother if she was Catholic, and they both laughed. He explained, "We have Mass daily, and every evening after the day's activities, the children will pray the Rosary and practice hymns for the next morning. They will not possibly have time to be taken elsewhere for Mass!"

My mother was elated. Three months later my sister and I found ourselves at an idyllic old farmhouse in the Alps, running barefoot up a dewy hill to the neighbor's cow barn to fetch milk for breakfast. The next morning, as I knelt on the creaky floor of a family house chapel with twenty other girls in long skirts, I realized without being told that this was the Mass of the Ages. The upstairs bedroom-turned-chapel, clouded with incense, reminded me of the first Mass, where another solemn group of friends watched as the Priest and Victim offered the Sacrifice of the New Covenant. When the young congregation bowed their veiled heads and sang the beautiful Sanctus of the Missa de Angelis, I knew that I had come home.

Afterwards at breakfast, I told my sister with all the eloquence of an excited 13-year-old, "This is what we've been looking for! These people are like us, except more!" When we returned home, I told my parents, who found the closest traditional parish. We started attending Mass and Catechesis there. The entire family had fallen in love with this Mass. I was especially struck by the beauty and worthiness of the music in the liturgy and returned with new fervor for the Gregorian chant and singing all the older hymns around the house. Though I was pitifully unskilled, the holiness of the prayers combined with the ancient melodies fascinated me.

On this path to the Traditional Latin Mass, I found many dear friends and treasured mentors. Through the Traditional Mass, I was meeting other young people who challenged me to actively work towards holiness. Later that year, I joined some friends from the parish in Catholic scouting (the International Union of Guides and Scouts of Europe). It was initially amazing to behold middle school and high school students kneeling in private prayer for thirty minutes after Holy Mass. At youth events, many of my friends stayed up late to finish their daily Rosaries. And could it really be true that my beloved kerchief and long dresses were considered "classic" and "chic?" I discovered with glee that these pious people understood jokes about the Baltimore Catechism and delighted in references to the lives of the saints. My insecurity about living my faith in the public sphere vanished with a rapidity surpassing even that of the abbreviated rosaries said by the Fatima children before the Blessed Mother appeared to them. With it disappeared my indifference, doubt, and even a great deal of social anxiety. Not only was the Catholic faith not merely a dated invention of my parents, but it was also a deep, overflowing font of 2000 years of studied and exquisitely beautiful tradition.

Many of these new peers played the organ or led choirs, so when the Covid-19 lockdowns came into effect, and our parish lost its weekly organist, I decided to learn how to play. It couldn't be difficult for a piano player to learn, I thought. Though I now recognize the naivete with which I approached the task, I thank God for it. I was able to receive a German diocesan scholarship to study organ and choir direction for three years, which in turn enabled me to start a girls' schola and later would qualify me to become a regular organist for a parish in Rome. I recently helped to start a new choir and am still continuing my formation in sacred music. I sincerely think that if it were not for the beauty and community I found in the Traditional Mass, I would never have developed this talent God has given me for His glory.

Much of adolescence is the discovery of one's place in the Church and society, and if it were not for the Traditional Latin Mass, I personally would have found this task significantly more difficult than it already necessarily is. It was truly the Traditional Latin Mass that gave me a home and a sense of belonging in the Church, which was critical in strengthening my faith and finding my Catholic identity. As a product of these graces, many new and wonderful opportunities for working in the Lord's vineyard have been opened to me, and I have built holy, lasting friendships with my fellow laborers. I firmly believe that it is the graces that have come to me through the Traditional Latin Mass that have made me a happier, holier person coming out of my teenage years. God has used the Latin Mass to "give joy to my youth." And that is why I am overwhelmed anew with such immense gratitude whenever I hear the murmured prayer at the beginning of Holy Mass: "Introíbo ad altáre Dei, ad Deum qui laetíficat iuventútem meam."

35. WHEREVER WE GO, THE MASS IS HOME
Anastasia, Age 16, New York

STAT CRUX DUM VOLVITUR ORBIS. THE CROSS stands while the world turns. This, the motto of the Carthusian order, describes my experience with the traditional Mass very well. Throughout my life I have experienced a great deal of change, as I have been moving constantly since I was very young, sometimes spending only six months in one place. Through all this, the one thing that has never changed, never left, has been the traditional Mass. I have always known that no matter what country I am in, no matter what the world outside looks like, the Mass, my Mass, will always be there. I will always be at home when I worship God. My life has been built around the Mass, for it is not only the liturgy of the Mass that I treasure, but the way of life and virtue it inspires. The pilgrim's path my parents set my tiny feet upon in my infancy I will follow 'til the journey's end.

I am what some people refer to as a "cradle trad," as I was born into Tradition. In fact, I have only been to the Novus Ordo twice in my life. My mother was raised in Tradition, and met my father at a traditional Mass. They committed to raising their children in Tradition as well. My parents struggled to find traditional Masses and would only move where there was a Latin Mass available. They have made many sacrifices to ensure that we always had the Latin Mass. Knowing of the great lengths they went to so that I could be a traditional Catholic makes me infinitely grateful to them for this incredible gift.

For as long as I can remember, the church has been a place of reverence. From the time you come into the sanctuary and genuflect, you are impressed by the fact that you are in the presence of Christ the King. The beautiful sacred music and artwork lift the heart and mind to God, and the candles and incense, coupled with the solemn respect of the celebrant and altar servers, are a constant reminder of the homage due to our King and Victim, truly present on the altar. I know that around me are my brothers and sisters *in Christo*, who love God as I do and wish also to come and adore Him in the Blessed Sacrament. The instant sense of belonging: that I am here, in the church, before my God, with others who wish to love Him in the most reverent way, is incredible. No matter what the country, or even continent, no matter the differences of language and culture that divide us, I truly feel at home with those who come to Mass with the familiar chapel veils, black leather-bound missals in hand, to honor our Savior.

My earliest memories of the Latin Mass find me in a small church in Kansas, surrounded by friends and neighbors. I received my First Communion in this parish, alongside many of my longtime friends. I can still see the gold and cream wallpaper in the sanctuary and the crucifixion scene above the altar. I had a very true feeling of home there. When I was six, we moved to Europe. We traveled here and there, attending Mass in some of the beautifully ornate churches and basilicas of Central Europe. Each church, no matter how great or humble, was home to me. Sienna, Venice, Rome, Salzburg, Assisi, Prague and Bologna: at each new church, the differences melted away as the familiar Latin words were spoken. I could sing with the choir in each place, as the *Missa Orbis Factor, Missa de Angelis, Missa Cum Jubilo*, and the other Masses of the liturgical year were just as familiar to me as the words of my own tongue.

When we moved to Madrid, Spain, our traditional parish was just down the road from our apartment, so we had the wonderful privilege of going to daily Mass. Mass was after dinner, and the evening lamp-lit walks with my mom led us three blocks away, down the stairs of an apartment building, and into our basement chapel, with its dropped ceilings and fluorescent lights. Although our kind parish priest, Don Oscar, never spoke English to me, his words were comfortingly familiar and welcome as he said Mass. Once again, I found home.

Eventually, we left Spain for Ireland, where our church was plain and stone; devoid of the marble floors, rich paintings, Baroque architecture, and awe-inspiring vaulted ceilings of our travels. The cold, impersonal, and weatherbeaten churches in the Land of Saints and Scholars starkly contrasted with the opulence of the continent. The piety of these Irish, however, who had fought so hard to bring back the liturgy of the Mass Rocks, glowed more brightly than the gilded statues of Bohemia or the *milagros* of Spain. The great Dominicans of the Church looked down on us from the stained glass windows in our Irish church, and the painted plaster angels on either side of the altar bowed in constant adoration.

When we moved back to the U. S., Mass was being said in an auditorium on the campus of our parish school. Despite my surroundings, which were comprised of folding chairs, foam kneelers, and HVAC ducts, I felt at home. My daily life again blessed by opportunities to serve God, I was very active in that parish. I was able to volunteer at our annual St. Joseph's Table and Parish Breakfast. I also attended Scripture classes taught by one of our priests.

A year ago, our family came to New York, and we now attend a small, over-capacity mission chapel that just celebrated its fortieth anniversary. Here also I feel at home. I am very active in this parish as well. I am a part of the choir and the Altar and Rosary Society, I clean the church monthly, and I have participated in many parish activities and projects since our arrival. I am very excited to play violin for a wedding in our parish and volunteer at a small summer camp next month. My life, full of service for God and activities in our traditional community, feels blessed and beautiful.

The Latin Mass has influenced my life and my plans, God willing, for the future, in a huge way. My six years of Latin are due to the beauty of the language of the Church. My Latin exams are the exams I prepare for the most each year, and the gold medals and accolades I have received in Latin are the awards I am most proud of. My love for doing ecclesiastical embroidery and art is also due, in many ways, to the Faith. As a small child, I often watched my mom working on and repairing vestments for the priests, and painting the parish Easter candle year after year. This beautiful work inspired me to begin ecclesiastical embroidery, which I enjoy very much. The music book I love the most is our big blue hymnal, and if one were to be a fly on the wall in our van on road trips, the songs you would hear would most likely be a two voice rendition of *O Gloriosa Virginum* and the *Ave Maria*, sung in rounds. Tradition has formed me my whole life; it is a great part of who I am as a person and as a Catholic. I am committed to modesty, and to the Catholic ideal of a homemaking wife and mother. I hope one day to raise a family for Christ, and to pass on to my children my love for and devotion to the Latin Mass.

Stat crux dum volvitur orbis. For me, the cross truly has stood, still and unchanging, amidst the many changes of my life. At the root of my every day stands the ancient Faith built on a rock, firm and unending, for did Christ not say, "Behold, I am with you all days, even to the consummation of the world"?

36. THE LATIN MASS BUILDS COMMUNITY
Margaret, Age 12, Wisconsin

I STARTED MY LIFE GOING TO THE NOVUS ORDO. Then we moved when I was 5. We were looking for a church to go to. When we visited my current church, I whispered to mom, "This is so pretty! We should join here." Since then, I always imagined that was why we went to my church. However, the real reason is that my dad fell in love with the Latin Mass while he was in college. I am going to write about how I came to love the Traditional Latin Mass (TLM) and why I love it so much.

When I was five what appealed to me were the statues and lights. At my church we have a Mary statue up front that is made from gold and I thought it was the loveliest thing in the world. The statues lining the walls are of the apostles. Each has gold on them and is carrying something that represents their life. For example St. Peter is holding keys. I also loved the chandeliers: they are gold and hang from the ceiling.

At the age of eight years old, I fell in love with the choir. A lot of TLM churches have a good choir. The Latin songs make them sound like angels. The choir at my church is very talented because they practice a lot. If you listen to the songs you can usually find where you are in the missal. An example is the Kyrie. The Kyrie is near the beginning of the Mass. The choir sings almost all of the high Masses at my church. The Sister Adorers of the Royal Heart of Jesus also sing sometimes.

Now that I am twelve, I have begun to love the reverence of the Mass and how it affects the people there to show reverence as well. First I would like to talk about the reverence I notice in the priest. The priest genuflects every time he crosses the tabernacle's path. This shows great reverence to the Holy Eucharist. The priest is solemn and focuses on the Mass. He also faces the tabernacle a great deal during the liturgy. The priest is very attentive to the prayers during the Mass and is very intentional about them. He also focuses on where he looks, how his hands are folded, and how he moves. This respect I love because you can almost not find it anywhere else.

My church is very blessed to have religious sisters in our community, who are very reverent. During the liturgy their eyes are attentive to either their missals or the priest. When they move at church they barely move, and when they do, they move slowly and very quietly. They are a solemn example to kids and adults alike, especially because the liturgy is so long.

The reverence by the lay people is stunning. At church most of the men and boys wear nice pants, collared shirts, and nice shoes. Most of the women and girls wear below the knee dresses or skirts, plain shirts that at least cover the shoulder, and they wear veils to imitate Our Lady. This reverent dressing is because we are in God's house. If little kids get fussy they are taken out of the church by their parents, which decreases the amount of crying in God's house. The older kids read the missal or listen to the choir, and try to not be distracted.

The liturgy and how people act there are different then their day to day lives. An example that I love is how people conduct themselves at the communion rail. As everyone goes up to communion they fold their hands. Each person gets closer to the front and waits until no one is in front of them, they will see a long kneeler. People kneel on the kneeler, if there is a cloth, they put their hands under the cloth, tip their head back, close their eyes and stick their tongue ¾'s of the way out. This shows respect and reverence to the Holy Eucharist especially by kneeling down because Jesus is King. You would kneel down in front of a king. When the Holy Eucharist is put in people's mouths there is no need to fear dropping Our Lord or having little crumbs on your hands. It shows great care for His precious body.

There are many other things I also love in the traditional Latin Mass. These include prayers, community, and the history of the materials used. The prayers of the mass are so beautiful that I cannot help but loving them. They are confusing at first, because the priest is saying them in Latin and I am reading them in English so it is easy to skip lines. There are many psalms which add to the amount of the Bible proclaimed in the Mass.

I also love the Latin Mass community that has formed. There are lots of young and old people who make up the community. Everyone knows at least 5 families. The kids are all friends. I only have a couple of friends who do not go to my church. Good Catholic friendships are very important for children and especially teenagers so they have good support and do not fall away from the faith. The religious sisters also help build community with the girls to help with good relationships by having a girls' group every first Saturday of the month. The group begins with Mass, then we eat breakfast together, one sister gives a talk on a saint and the virtues they had, finally we do a craft which differs by age group. The priests are also part of the community. For example ICKSP is a religious order that offers the Latin Mass and offers things like a children's summer camp (which is really fun and religious) and a lay order. The families that attend the TLM are part of the community. During Mass people's friends help with kids and babies by looking after them as needed. They also do meal trains which are very helpful to new moms and people mourning. During all of the seasons people gather after Mass. At my church in winter we gather in the church basement and in the summer at a nearby park. Even if someone does not go downstairs or the park, they normally end up talking to friends on the way out the door. People stay a long time at both the park and basement. In the basement, people usually stay for 2 hours unless they are going to a friend's house. At the park, there are times when people stay from 2-6 hours!

I also appreciate the objects used in the Traditional Latin Mass and the history behind them. I am just now learning about the history of the TLM, but once I pick up a book about it I cannot put it down! The altar has to be there because if you are going to have a sacrifice you must have an altar. Did you know that the altar ledge (the raised part at the back of the altar where the candles get put) was not original? The candles used to be put on the floor near the altar. The part behind the altar that is very tall is called the canopy or throne. That was also not original. An altar should be made out of stone, but if it is made of wood there must be a stone in the altar that is big enough to hold the chalice and paten. The stone has relics in it. The chalice and paten are also interesting. The chalice must be made of gold or silver, but if it is silver its inside has to be gold. There is a white cloth made of linen that is three layers thick. It is used to soak up the precious blood if it should spill, which shows respect to God.

In summary, I love the Traditional Latin Mass's physical beauty, choir, community, reverence, and the history of the items used. The intricate detail of the statues and artwork, the awe inspiring dedication of the choir, which fills the church with music, the charity and friendliness of the people that form strong friendships and the reverence of the mass have all helped me on my journey to appreciate the TLM. As you can see the TLM grows with you. When you start your journey it is about exterior things, like the statues and people, but it becomes about an interior prayer life. Everyone will be different on how they grow but each will hopefully end with deep spiritual growth.

37. WHY YOUNG CATHOLICS DEVOTE THEMSELVES TO THE TRADITIONAL LATIN MASS
Evelyn, Age 12, Illinois

MY FAMILY DRIVES AN HOUR AND FIFTEEN minutes regularly every Sunday to get to Springfield Illinois. It has nothing to do with the city. It has to do with what's within it! We attend Traditional Latin Mass (TLM) regularly at Sacred Heart church. It's a bit of a long haul, considering six kids ages ranging from two months to twelve years old. But we all know (or those of us who are old enough to understand anyway) that it's completely worth it. The beautiful TLM, the Catholic liturgy in its most perfect form, is worth it. Really though, we would still be going to the Novus Ordo if my dad hadn't found us our parish, or if Covid hadn't come. Anyway, let me tell you our story.

My family began attending the Traditional Latin Mass in 2020, when our diocese and local parishes were shut down. My dad knew watching Mass on a screen wasn't the best he could do for our souls, Covid or no Covid, so he scoured the area for open churches. One of the closest open parishes near us was Sacred Heart, run by the Canons of St. John Cantius. We had been to the Canons' church in Chicago, and my parents were fascinated by the beauty of the TLM. I was too young to notice anything other than the magnificent church (and so were my siblings). Now this was mostly sheer coincidence when my dad found this church. All he was looking for was an open parish he could take his four children (at the time) and his wife to. He wasn't looking for anything fancy.

If you are wondering why in the world you would want to go to a Mass that's a whole fifteen minutes to a half hour longer, then here's why. First of all, it's more reverent and God centered. If you have ever been to a TLM, you might have noticed that the priest is not facing the people, he's facing the tabernacle. This is an outward sign indicating that the Mass and what the priest is doing is entirely an offering to God, and not directed at all towards the people. The people are simply there to worship, and nothing else.

Secondly, the TLM is the Catholic liturgy in its complete fullness. If you look at the prayers from the Novus Ordo and the TLM, you might notice that some of the prayers in the TLM are missing, or even changed, in the Novus Ordo. Take the *Confiteor* for example. In the beginning of the Confiteor in the Novus Ordo, the priest and the people confess to God together. In the TLM, the priest confesses to God first, which cleanses himself, uniting himself to Jesus, so he can worthily give the people absolution of venial sins. This is a small example. Also, looking at the TLM Confiteor, it pleads the intercession of more holy angels and saints rather than the Novus Ordo Confiteor, which only addresses God, Mary, and my "brothers and sisters."

One can't mention the TLM without its beautiful music, Gregorian Chant. Gregorian chant has lived on for many, many, many years, and is sung throughout the TLM. You might have heard of the *Salve Regina* or the *Regina Caeli*, both Marian hymns. Gregorian chant is often sung by monks or nuns, or by a schola. Prayers chanted in the TLM are the Gloria, the Sanctus, and more.

A good way to catch on to the TLM is to follow along in a missal. In my opinion, it is easiest to follow along to the *Gloria* when it is being chanted. Overall, it is easier to pay attention during a High Mass than a Low Mass, but you can pray by yourself when most of the prayers aren't sung. High Masses are more filled with chanting, but Low Masses are still as reverent and God-centered. If you have trouble following along, listen to the breathtaking music, or watch the priest and the altar servers as they say or assist Mass. I'm not making any promises, but TLM churches are usually very pretty, or at least have a lot of statues. You can just look at them, and pray. You could even pray the Rosary. That is a benefit of the TLM being said almost entirely in Latin.

Another wonder of the TLM is the altar rail. The altar rail insists that you receive in the most reverent way possible: kneeling, and on the tongue. It also ensures that no one who wishes to receive it kneeling and on the tongue will be denied the Eucharist, and that that most people will receive on the tongue, generally preventing any particle of the Eucharist from falling to the ground, or being stepped on, or even touching someone's hand. People's hands are everywhere. Changing diapers, taking out the trash, etc., at the end of the day, your hands have been a lot of places that you probably don't want the God of the world, your Savior, the one who created everything, to touch. "Well, how is my tongue any better than my hands?", you ask. The answer is, the Eucharist is going straight from the priest's hand, to your mouth, eliminating almost all chance of the Eucharist touching the floor. To add, if you were baptized in the Traditional Rite, then exorcised salt was put in your mouth, blessing it.

There is also beauty in the fact that most women who regularly attend the TLM wear veils. Veils are a sign that under the veil is something beautiful, something sacred. The tabernacle is veiled, and it is extremely sacred. Another reason women veil is for a personal devotion to Jesus Christ.

The TLM has affected me personally in multiple ways. I have attended more special Masses since then, like the Rorate Caeli and Candlemas. It has led me into a deeper understanding of our Catholic faith and what it is supposed to look like, how we are supposed to try to get the very best we can for our souls, and show God in multiple ways that we love Him whether we have to drive more than desired or not. I think the driving has been good for my family and I because it sanctifies our Sunday, and really dedicates it to Jesus.

To conclude, the Traditional Latin Mass is beautiful, reverent, and perfect. It is the original form of the Catholic liturgy. I hope that this writing has inspired you to start receiving on the tongue, or even attending a TLM parish. My family and I have grown to love the Traditional Latin Mass because of all that it offers: truth, beauty, and one day, eternal happiness in Heaven. We hope that everyone everywhere is exposed to its beauty, and grows to love it as much, or even more, than we do.

38. DISCOVERING THE ANCIENT MASS THROUGH AN ACCIDENT
Eleanor, Age 17, Wisconsin

WHEN I WAS THREE YEARS OLD, I GASHED MY head on our dinner table and had to go to the hospital to get stiches. It was a Saturday night, my dad was gone, and our family was in the habit of going to a Novus Ordo Mass on those nights to fulfil our Sunday obligation. Since we clearly couldn't make it that night, my mom reached out to one of her friends who went to the Latin Mass. She said that there was a Latin Mass at 5:30 PM on Sunday. It was a convenient time for my mom, so we decided to go to it. She immediately fell in love with it and knew that this Mass was what she had been searching for all her life. We decided to keep going to it and we got connected with some wonderful Traditional Catholic families. Both priests that we had during the span of about 4-5 years were wonderful, and they helped us continued to grow in our faith. Through the good example of our friends, we discovered the importance of veiling in the presence of the Blessed Sacrament, and dressing in a modest way all the time—something which I am so grateful for!

I do not know where I would be today regarding my faith if we had not discovered the Latin Mass. Though I did not see the real value and beauty of the Extraordinary Form of the Mass whether it was a High or Low one, over the past few years I have grown to deeply appreciate and love it. From the organ music to the polyphonic music, to the Gregorian chant, and the beauty of the Mass itself—it all brings such peace to my mind and soul and focuses my mind on heavenly things. I find that I have more time to meditate and that it is easier to do so when attending the Extraordinary Form of the Mass; something which I cannot do much when I attend a Novus Ordo one since there's almost always something being spoken out loud, and it's all in English. Yes, a lot of things are still spoken out loud in the Latin Mass, but I can still pray and meditate when they are being sung or spoken. For instance, since I have a missal, I can read the different parts of the Mass and know what's being said by the priest or sung by the choir; but once I'm finished reading it, I can pray more if the priest or choir is not finished with that part yet. I can only do this because it is in a language which I cannot fluently speak. Another thing is that after the *Sanctus* and *Benedictus* have been sung, the prayers leading up to and during the Consecration are said in a whisper by the priest. This allows me to pray, contemplate and adore Jesus silently in the most Holy Eucharist who I am about to receive into my heart for a longer period of time than I could if I was at a Novus Ordo Mass. Yes, the words of the Consecration are the most important thing in the Mass, but it is directed solely towards God, and it does not really matter if we hear it or not.

I do not believe that it is wrong to go to the Ordinary Form of the Mass, and I do not believe that it is invalid; but I see the Extraordinary Form of the Mass as being *far* superior to it. Every time I attend the New Mass (even though our priests say it very reverently), I can only describe it as feeling empty. Yes, it is wonderful to be able to receive Jesus in the most Holy Eucharist which is the center of the Mass and the most important thing, but it's missing so many beautiful prayers and chants which render the Mass more fruitful to the soul. I do not believe that if you don't go to the Latin Mass, you are a bad Catholic; but for me, my faith would not mean as much if I had no access to a Latin Mass.

This past Holy week, we had the great blessing of going to the pre-55 Triduum. The church was almost two and a half hours away and we had to stay in an Airbnb, but I do not regret one bit of it! The Mass on Holy Thursday with the three priests was so beautiful! I loved singing the *Pange Lingua* during the procession to the Altar of Repose. It was all so peaceful and beautiful, and the candles and lilies on the steps leading up to the Altar of Repose created a most wonderful effect! One of the parts of the Good Friday Liturgy that really touched my heart was during the procession. The women in the choir were singing a beautiful version of the *Vexilla Regis*. As the servers, priests and seminarians were processing through the church while it was being sung, for the first time in my life, I truly felt like I was at a funeral (as it ought to, since it was the greatest funeral that ever took place or ever will take place). As I gazed on the Cross which was being carried in the procession, I was moved to tears recalling that *I* was the cause of Christ's passion and death; it was because of *my* sins that he suffered so intensely both in body and soul and died in such cruel agony. Another thing that was very powerful to me during the Good Friday Liturgy was at the veneration of the Cross. Instead of having the Cross held up by the priest and one or two of the servers, they laid it on the ground resting on one of the steps leading up to the altar. It is hard to describe what I felt as I approached the Cross, but it made me reflect on the infinite humility which Jesus underwent during his passion and death.

Looking back to that time, the way I can describe it is that it helped me understand more clearly that yes, He offered Himself up entirely to God for the sake of my salvation. I was already fully aware of this, but I did not understand it more fully until then. I regretfully say this, but before this time, I had never kissed the feet of Jesus with so much love and sorrow for my sins; but I am also extremely thankful that this time He gave me the grace to kiss His sacred feet with so much sorrow and love.

The Easter Vigil was so glorious! Though it was about four and a half hours long, it was so worth it! There are doors on the High Altar which are closed during Lent and only opened on great feast days during that time. At the Gloria while the bells were being rung at the Easter Vigil Mass, the doors are slowly opened revealing a great statue of Our Lady (who the church is dedicated to) holding the Infant Jesus in her arms. Everything from the three priests with their gold-colored vestments, to the music being played and the doors being opened on the High Altar overwhelmed me to such an extent that it brought me to tears. It was truly a glorious Mass. Though I have never experienced a Novus Ordo Triduum before, I cannot believe that any could be equal in beauty and fruitfulness to the one I experienced this past year.

I have never heard the music in which you are enveloped during the Latin Mass in a Novus Ordo Mass unless it has been one at the Shrine where we attend Mass. Some of the choir members like to sing Traditional hymns and chants during the weekday English Masses, which is such a blessing and refreshment! I'm so grateful that the music that is sung during a Latin Mass is more interesting than the ones that are sung at a Novus Ordo Mass, and that there are multiple melodies for the Ordinary of the Mass. It would get so repetitive for me to hear the exact same *Kyrie, Gloria, Sanctus* and *Agnus Dei* every time I go to Mass. I still believe that it pleases God, but the other variations for the Ordinary of the Mass are so beautiful! I have nothing against singing hymns, but the ones I always hear when I go to an English Mass are far inferior to those which I hear at a Latin Mass. In the Extraordinary Form of the Mass, the Sacred music and hymns which are sung have beautiful melodies and have more than one part to them as well which makes them more interesting and beautiful. The Traditional hymns and Polyphonic music which I have been immersed in during my years of attending the Latin Mass always raise my heart and mind to God. It makes my soul soar up to heaven, especially when the right dynamics are added into them. It brings such peace and tranquility to my soul since its focus is on God and Our Blessed Mother. If I am not singing in the choir, I sing the music in my heart which brings great peace and joy into my soul.

The Latin Mass has affected my life in such a positive way that I have no intention of giving it up, even if I could only attend it in secret. Though we may not always see it, I firmly believe that everything works together for our good as was evident when I gashed my head. It was certainly not an ideal thing, but God used that accident to bring us to the Latin Mass and discover its beauty. I am so grateful for all He has done for me through the Roman Rite of the Mass even though I did not see the fruits of it at first.

Praised be Jesus, Mary and Joseph, now and forever! Deo gratias!

39. LATE HAVE I LOVED THEE
Hannah, Age 18, Michigan

"LATE HAVE I LOVED YOU, O BEAUTY EVER ancient and ever new! Late have I loved you!" These words of Saint Augustine perfectly describe my love for the Latin Mass. Of all the events I have experienced in my life, attending the Latin Mass every Sunday has been the one thing that constantly deepens my desire to know the truth. Every gesture and word of the Tridentine Rite, the beauty of the many churches I've attended, and the sacred music that often accompanies the Mass all raise one's heart, mind, and soul to Truth Himself. The Latin Mass sparks an awe within me that has grown into a deep desire to draw closer to Our Lord, and through Him to know the truth.

I have been attending the Latin Mass for nearly my entire life. My father, a convert to Catholicism, has been deeply in love with the Tridentine Rite ever since he first discovered it, and he has always shared his love of the Mass with me. We moved to Detroit, Michigan in 2007, and shortly after joined the vibrant Latin Mass community that has been growing in the city since the indult of Pope John Paul II. As I grew and matured, I came to realize the differences between the Tridentine Rite and the Novus Ordo, and I noticed that the Latin Mass always raised my heart and mind closer to God than did the English Mass. When I attended the Latin Mass on Sundays, I could feel the True Presence of Christ in the church, and this feeling was assisted by the reverence of the priests, altar boys, and parishioners, as well as the majestic beauty of the Romanesque-style church that I attend. Every aspect of the Mass, from the incense and prayers to the music and church architecture, stirred something within my heart. I longed to love God more, and I desired to seek the truth about Him and the world He created. This longing has increased as I continue to mature in my Faith, and as I get older I continue to try to draw closer to Truth Himself every day.

One of the reasons why the Latin Mass makes me desire to seek the truth is the significance of every word and gesture of the liturgy. All of the prayers said by the priest during the Mass have a special meaning, as do all of the little gestures he makes; without these the liturgy would be incomplete. For example, during the Canon of the Mass, the priest makes several small signs of the Cross over the bread and wine. After the consecration, he makes five signs of the Cross over the newly consecrated Body and Blood of Christ, which represent the five wounds of Our Lord. Later, the priest makes five more signs of the Cross with the Body and Blood. The first three ("Per ipsum, et cum ipso, et in ipso . . . ") represent the three hours during which Jesus hung on the Cross; the last two ("est tibi Deo Patri omnipotenti, in unitate Spiritus Sancti . . . ") represent the separation of Christ's Body and Soul when He died. If so many small words and gestures are necessary in the worship of God, then surely He must really be Goodness, Beauty, and Truth Itself. This significance of every word and gesture is the reason why the structure of the liturgy leads me to desire to seek the truth every time I witness the Latin Mass.

Music also deepens my desire to know the truth, particularly sacred music and Gregorian chant. I have been singing in my parish choir for six years, and the experience of learning sacred polyphony and chant has shaped both my spiritual and secular life. In the Tridentine liturgy, a great emphasis is placed on polyphony and chant as having pride of place in the musical life of the Church. My parish choir is directed by our pastor, Fr. Eduard Perrone, who was one of the last to graduate from the nationally renowned Palestrina Institute before its closing in 1968. Under Fr. Perrone's instruction, I have been privileged to learn a wide range of musical works from the broad repertoire of polyphony that has been handed down to us through the centuries. I have also been able to participate in the women's chant schola, and have directed the schola on certain occasions.

Recently I joined a semi-professional choir that sings once a month for First Fridays, under the direction of another brilliant conductor, Wassim Sarweh. His choir focuses primarily on Renaissance polyphony, such as the works of Palestrina and Victoria. Singing with both of these choirs not only grants a wealth of experience, but it also contributes to a greater participation in the celebration of the Mass. I remember singing Franz Biebl's *Ave Maria* at First Friday one month, with only eight other choir members. There is no other word to describe it other than heavenly. The harmonies blended together and wove around each other in such a way that you could feel the music, and we were all truly praying the *Ave Maria* as we sang. Music such as Biebl's *Ave Maria*, Palestrina's many works, and Gregorian chant all raise the heart, mind, and soul to God. Once we are raised to the contemplation of His glory, desire to seek Him more cannot be far away. Sacred music leads to a strong desire for truth, beauty, and goodness. We do not always recognize this longing, but it is there nevertheless. Music is so beautiful that it often transcends human comprehension, and when we cannot fully understand something, we desire to seek it out more and learn the full truth of it.

Each one of these factors of the Latin Mass contributes to a deepening of my desire to know the truth. My father's love of the Tridentine Rite made me grow to love the Mass from a young age; the structure and significance of the liturgy as well as traditional church architecture both raise my mind and heart to a greater contemplation of God, Who is Truth; and the experience of singing and hearing sacred polyphony and chant has led me to a deeper love for the Mass, for Christ, and for Goodness, Truth, and Beauty. The Latin Mass truly is a "Beauty ever ancient and ever new." Being able to experience it at least once in a lifetime is a gift, but having the privilege of attending the Latin Mass every Sunday is a great blessing. Without the Latin Mass, I doubt that I would be where I am today, and I doubt that I would have a desire to continue seeking the truth in everything I do. To quote Saint Augustine once more, "Late have I loved you, O Beauty ever ancient and ever new! Late have I loved you! And, behold, you were within me, and I out of myself, and there I searched for you."

40. TRULY TRANSFORMATORY
Francis, Age 15, California

I CONCRETELY REMEMBER MY FIRST EXPERIENCE attending the Tridentine Mass. It was the 16th of October 2022, I had finally managed to convince my dad to transport me there, at St. Vitus Catholic Church in San Fernando, despite the lengthy journey. Until that time, I had recently begun regularly attending Mass and going to English Masses at St. John Chrysostom in Inglewood, California. However, my first exposure to the Traditional Mass was definitely one of the most profound mystical experiences I have encountered in my life, something truly transformatory in the way I viewed the true worship of the Triune God. One of the first things I noticed were, the widespread reverence and warmness of the community, for me it did not seem like an entirely foreign culture I would have difficulty adapting too, rather a people who were captivated with the traditions of the church, entirely devoting themselves to prayer and contemplation, in sufficient preparation for the Holy Sacrifice of the Mass. In spite of the Mass being held outside, within a tent, a mystery of awe and wonder prevailed in the space as if God had truly dwelled among these people. Having altar served for the Ordinary Form beforehand, I already possessed a general sense of how we are supposed to behave, act, and perform duties within the sanctuary. Unfortunately, many acolytes in the modern church have not preserved a reverent sense of the sacred in this manner, and I have personally witnessed this. However, at the Traditional Mass, I recognized that any laxed attitude was totally absent, that the altar servers, being sufficiently trained, were able to aid in divine worship, through their own reverence, and honor for God within the Holy of Holies. As the Holy Mass began, the organ ramped up, a solemn procession headed towards the altar, an Introit chant had started to be sung by the choir, and the pleasant smell of incense conquered our surroundings. I was totally overwhelmed with the theocentric ordering of this Mass. There was no introductory dialogue, or the use of modern instruments, perceived to be engaging with the people. Rather, it was completely understood by everyone that the liturgy is established and ordered to God (theocentric), and not to us the people (anthropocentric).

It is indeed said that the liturgy is the greatest catechetical tool, and I believe that the Traditional Mass is instrumental and crucial to help us understand the true nature of the Mass.

Throughout my life, and doubtless the lives of countless other Catholics, I understood Sunday Mass to be a "gathering of the people of God" in order to offer praise and adoration to the Lord of hosts. While in this does bear some degree of truth, what happened to traditional Catholic theology and doctrine on the institution of the perpetual sacrifice at the Last Supper, and of the New Covenant ministerial Priesthood? The Council of Trent gives us substantial teaching on the Holy Sacrifice of the Mass in Session XXII, Chapter I. While most Catholics may understand that within the Mass, the bread and wine truly, really, and substantially become the Body, Blood, Soul, and Divinity of Our Lord Jesus Christ, how many know that the Mass is the perfect unbloody perpetuation of the same sacrifice of Calvary, Christ offered to the Father? How many know that the same merits of Christ's sacrifice are renewed and applied to us today, each time the Mass is celebrated?

The Traditional Mass has assisted in my deeper learning of the true nature of the liturgy, simply through emphasizing the supreme focus on the majesty of our Creator, and the restlessness of man without God, that man is sinful and entirely helpless without divine saving grace. This is especially expressed in the "Prayers at the Foot of the Altar," consisting of Psalm 42, Confiteor, and a final plea for mercy. While to the modern liturgical eye, these might seem repetitive, excessive, or even scrupulous, the truth is quite the contrary. Rather, they point to the fact that even a priest, whose hands are consecrated for divine service, is nevertheless bitterly unworthy to even be at the helm of Christ's sanctuary, and therefore pleads repeatedly that he be made whole and clean, to offer up the sacrifice of the Mass. This same attitude is reflected throughout the Traditional Mass, the traditional *Munda Cor Meum* prayer before the Gospel, the Offertory prayers of *Suscipe Sancte Pater*, *In spiritu humilitatis*, and *Suscipe Sancte Trinitas*, the three prayers of the celebrant before his communion, and even after the reception of the Sacrament, a profound thanksgiving unto God is also emphasized. While under modern Catholic culture, we are taught that Sunday Mass is a casual exercise, something ordinary and habitual, the Traditional Mass by its very nature and strict rubricism, catechizes us that the Mass is a supreme spiritual encounter with God, and requires our full attention and participation, not merely by vocal expressions, but by intense interior contemplation.

I am extremely grateful for my personal experiences with the Traditional Mass, and for its profound impact on my spiritual life, and my knowledge of the faith. It didn't stop with the Fraternity of St. Peter at St. Vitus! After a few months, I was able to visit a Traditional mass done by a religiously orthodox order in the Catholic Church in California almost a year after I had visited St. Vitus. It seems I was captivated by the same mysteries as I was being an infant to the rite almost a year back. I was enraptured by a thorough sense of authentic full-bodied traditional Catholicism. The choir had sung the Mass exquisitely with sacred chant and sacred polyphony, allowing the congregation and people of God to immerse ourselves in the mystery of God, the beatific vision, and his saints. The Mass, being of course incorporated with the liturgical costumes of the same religious order, gave me a real sense of connecting the liturgy with the history of the saints who attended and met the Lord in the same Mass. It consoles me knowing that this is the same Mass that for over a millennia, (the structure being established already by Pope Gregory the Great in the 6th century AD), this was the same Mass that thousands of saints revered and worshiped God in. This was, at least fundamentally, the same Mass that St. Francis of Assisi (my personal favorite saint), had attended, and it was indeed within this Mass he preached upon the doctrine of the Real Presence. This was the same Mass that St. Francis de Sales, St. Phillip Neri, and St. Charles Borromeo celebrated in their zealous renewal of the Catholic Religion. While liturgical revisionists make assertions that diminish the liturgical history and foundation of the Traditional Mass, it is important to realize that countless generations and peoples made themselves accustomed to this same liturgy, and the exclusivity of the Latin language did not serve as a barrier from active participation, indeed it actually increased their devotion in the sacrifice of the Mass, and the same doubtless has been the case for many young people like myself, who are searching and yearning for something beyond their own mundane daily lives, to serve as a ladder to God's grace and love, which he dispensed to us when he gave us Our Lord, his only son, to redeem the human race from sin.

Lastly, the Traditional Mass has aided me personally in appreciating to a greater degree the rich musical traditions of the Latin Church, especially with Gregorian Chant. During the Liturgy, it brings me joy to praise God singing, for example, the Gloria from *Missa de Angelis* or *Credo IV*. These ancient chants also tie back to how over centuries, and all over the world, we as a Catholic people are singing the same hymns in praise and adoration of God. Thus, the Traditional Mass is a great inheritance of our shared liturgical tradition, a heritage that ought not to be swiftly discarded out of fear of disunity within the church, but rather it should be boldly uplifted with righteous pride.

41. A MASS THAT WAS NEVER-CHANGING
Kateri, Age 15, California

I HAVE BEEN GOING TO THE TRADITIONAL LATIN Mass for several years now, and with good reason. It has enriched me spiritually in many ways, and I have felt a stronger love for Jesus Christ in my soul than ever before.

This is my story:

When I was younger, only about five years old, I went to the Novus Ordo Mass every Sunday. My older brother, especially, instilled in me a love for God and for Holy Mass. He told me to meditate on the Mass, and the sacrifice that was taking place, and to spend lots of time contemplating the decades of the rosary. But to be honest, I never understood how the Mass was a "sacrifice". At my Novus Ordo church, the priests said it was a *celebration*. To my younger and smaller self, I had trouble figuring out whether the Mass was a sacrifice or a celebration. Because to me, it certainly could not have been both. A celebration reminded me of parties and happiness, and a sacrifice reminded me of sorrow and pain. A small child does not understand the meaning of true sorrow and deep pain, and so the concept of a "sacrifice" seemed very mysterious to me. I wondered a lot about it, but after not figuring out what a sacrifice really was, I decided to cast those thoughts aside. If I didn't understand it, then surely it wasn't important, right?

I lived in a similar way for years, trying to love God but not knowing what loving God really was. Trying to pay attention to Mass, but not understanding what was taking place. I knew God was present, but I didn't know any of the prayers. When did the bread become the Holy Eucharist? I used to think it was when the Novus Ordo band started singing the Holy, Holy, Lord God of Hosts and we all knelt. I even thought that I was already a saint, and that everyone around me was too. Hell was a place reserved for very, very few people, I thought.

As I got older, I started disliking Mass. Why did we have to go *every week*, sometimes even more frequently than that? I especially disliked when Christmas Day fell on a Saturday, because then we would have to go to Mass two days in a row. I noticed no difference in my spiritual life. I didn't even know what a spiritual life was. I was told by my brother and mother that it was something very special.

But I never knew what it was exactly. How can someone tell if they are advancing in their spiritual life? Since I had felt no change my entire life, I assumed I had reached that point of spiritual perfection long ago. But the saints loved the Mass very much, so if I was a saint, then how come I didn't like Mass?

One day, though, everything changed. My father announced that we were not going to our regular parish that Sunday, but to a different one. A different parish with a different Mass. It was all very mysterious to me.

When we arrived, I noticed how quiet it was. How sacred it felt. When the Traditional Latin Mass began to be celebrated in front of me, I was confused. I didn't understand a thing, and I didn't give anyone the sign of peace. It felt very different. I remember particularly disliking kneeling a lot and not being able to talk to people in the pews behind me. It was like something very serious was going on. But I had never thought the Mass to be very serious, so why was everyone so prayerful and reverent? And everyone dressed nice too. It wasn't like a get-together for everyone to join hands and sing happy songs and chat. It was a beautiful, sacred prayer.

For about the first six months I disliked both Masses. I didn't like kneeling for so long. The Novus Ordo Mass was boring enough, why did we have to go to a different Mass that felt twice as long?

Changes in my soul were slow, but definitely there. Over the years, I learned more and more. I learned that the Mass was a prayer, something I had never known before. I followed along to the prayers in the 1962 Missal and saw people reverently beating their chest at the Agnus Dei, and it seemed so interesting to do that, so I started doing that too. I wore a veil, which obscured some of my sight, making me almost see in tunnel-vision forward toward the altar. The Gregorian chants were breathtaking, and I would just kneel there, listening to the beautiful music and watch the incense float up to heaven, and I felt peace. I went from a child continuously asking her mother when we could leave, to a child who somehow just *knew* that she had to be silent. I learned, from the grace of God, that Mass is for praying. Mass is for adoring Christ. When I genuflected in front of the Altar, I really meant it. If I didn't walk slowly and reverently through the church, I felt like I was disrespecting God's holy place. Because God was there, and I knew it very well.

I started looking forward to Mass, and to the rosary, unlike ever before. I would take every moment to deeply meditate and pray. I would impatiently wait in the car on the drive to Mass, thinking about kneeling before the altar and pouring out my entire heart to God. He became my confidante, and so easily, like God's grace was aiding me, I would feel infinitely better after praying. It was like a breath of fresh air. When I was a child, I thought God was just this important god that made the world then took a step back. After going to the Latin Mass, I realized how much of a father He is. He did not take a step back from the world, and He listens to our prayers every day. I can lay total trust in Him because I know He loves me.

Sometimes I would envision the altar as a throne, and when the priest was consecrating the Eucharist, a king would come and sit on the throne. And at communion, the people were coming to the foot of the throne to beg their king for help, to adore their king and his mightiness, to thank their king for all he has done for them. It was truly special. But, in my mind, people could not go visit their king without a gift! Therefore, it would make sense that people had to *give* something to God when they went to receive, because God was giving Himself to them. The person receiving needed to have a desire for God and had to be as pure and sinless as possible. A person had to become like an angel from heaven before they could dare receive God.

As I grew older, I grew alongside a Mass that was never-changing. One that reflected the never-changing nature of God. It became like a home to me. I grew spiritually in ways I cannot even describe.

When I turned fourteen, I traveled to Spain for three months. Spain is an incredible place, really, and I had an amazing time there. But of course, everyone experiences the regular feelings of homesickness for the first week or so. I had never been in Europe before, so it was a very new experience to me.

One of the first things I noticed was my homesickness, and the desire for something familiar. On Sunday I went with my family to the Latin Mass in Madrid, and it patched up my homesick heart. When I knelt there, I poured my heart out to God in contemplative prayer, and I was more than glad that I was not at a Novus Ordo Mass. I didn't have to respond to prayers aloud or greet people. I could just pray and feel God's presence. The Traditional Latin Mass was a piece of home, but not like if I were to go to an American restaurant in Spain or see American tourists. What made it feel like home was God. That sacred presence in my church at home was there. That infinite peace, and the feeling of God's grace coaxing you into deep prayer so delicately. It was all there.

I'm sorry to say, but when I went to a Novus Ordo Mass in Spain, it wasn't the same. I tried very, very hard to feel the same, but it was so hard. The Mass was too distracting! I could not pray, or prepare myself for communion, or give thanksgiving afterward. I kept telling myself I would save my prayers and my devotions for after Mass, in the period of silence before the candles are blown out and the altar is disassembled. But that defeats the entire purpose of Mass! How can you go to a Mass and tell yourself that you will pray *afterward*? Mass is a prayer itself. How can you pray Mass after Mass is done? I went to the Novus Ordo Mass everyday in Spain except on Sundays (when we went to the Latin Mass), and I became confused again and again. I didn't feel at peace or at home at the Novus Ordo Mass. I had been going to the Novus Ordo for half of my life and yet it didn't feel at all like home. Not even nostalgic. All I could think was how I wished I could just be in the Latin Mass at that moment.

I've even gotten to the point where I stand in the pew in a Novus Ordo Mass and a particular thought runs through my mind. I don't try to think about anything but the Mass, yet, unbidden, this thought keeps returning: Why does this feel so fake? Why am I even here? What am I getting from this?

The only thing that consoles me at a Novus Ordo Mass is receiving the Holy Eucharist. But otherwise, I feel that childhood boredom I had felt for many years in the past. That wishing for it to be over soon.

I cannot fully explain why the Latin Mass has helped me so much. When someone asks me to explain my experience, I'm usually at a loss for words at first. How can you describe the deep movements of your soul in words? It truly is a very beautiful experience, and one a person can only understand after they have been to the Latin Mass themselves. I proudly say that I will try my very best to attend the Latin Mass as long as it remains available, for the rest of my life if God wills it. I believe that the Latin Mass is the Mass that will truly aid me on the journey to spiritual perfection. And I believe that it will change your life too, just as it did mine.

42. THE LATIN MASS AS THE CHURCH'S UNA VOCE
Bailey, Age 18, Ohio

Growing up, even at my Catholic school, my family was considered to be one of the "more religious" Catholic families. However, we merely fulfilled the minimum of attending Mass every Sunday at our Novus Ordo parish, participating in all of the common parish activities, and attending a private 'Catholic' school. I was around 10 years old when I started noticing that the families I was around at school and Church did not share a common understanding of what being Catholic actually meant. For them it did not include attending Sunday Mass or receiving the sacraments. In addition, I noticed many of my friends' parents started getting divorced and promoting fundraisers in our school that supported pro-choice organizations. Even at ten years old, I could not get over the fact that many of the people I knew that label themselves as Catholics did not seem to live out the teachings of the Church. My parents were also wary that our parish and school community had lost its strong faith. Homilies had turned from Aquinas and reflection on readings to five-minute, feel-good chit-chats between the priest and the congregation; families disappeared from Sunday mass until we were practically the only young family left in our parish. These are just a few aspects that started Dad on a journey that ended at an FSSP parish in downtown Dayton.

Up until a few weeks prior to my first Traditional Latin Mass, I was completely ignorant of the fact that the Mass was still being said in Latin at all. As far as I knew, Latin was a dead language that was for some odd reason still considered the language of the Church (although ten-year-old me saw no connection between the Novus Ordo Liturgy and the Latin Language apart from the occasional reference of 'Ave Maria'). When Dad first told me that he planned to take me to a Latin mass, while I expected the language to be different, I was not prepared for how different the experience would be from every other Mass I had ever attended.

When I first walked into the Church, I was struck with a sense of reverence. The building was a gorgeous cruciform Byzantine style Church which made it seem like a Cathedral compared to the modern, triangular Church I had attended for my whole life. It was clear that this building was not intended for socializing and catching up with your friends. This was a place where Christ was truly present Body, Blood, Soul, and Divinity. Everyone around me was kneeling in silent prayer; all I remember thinking was that I was in a Church full of very holy people.

I had always found it strange that, while we were always told that it is good to spend quiet one-on-one time with the Lord, the moment that Sunday Mass concluded many either would rush out or start talking while still in the Church. This did not happen when I went to the Traditional Latin Mass, and it made a big impression on me. The silence I experienced even during the Mass (this first TLM happened to be a Low Mass) caused me to really come out of my comfort zone. I could no longer drown out the quiet voice inside calling me to humble myself in mental prayer. It was through this profound silence that I was able to recognize the areas of my life where I needed to improve and ask for the strength to do it. At that Mass I learned the importance of quiet prayer, recognizing that if I wanted to live out my faith, I needed to allow myself to be still and hear Christ's voice.

In addition to the silence of the Mass, I was also rather confused as to why the priest was facing away from the congregation. Wasn't it his job to make sure that the congregation was fully participating in the liturgy? How was He supposed to fulfill that duty if I couldn't even hear what he was saying? I had been used to attending Masses where the priest would very often take a very casual approach to the liturgy. It never had occurred to me to question why, if Christ was the most important person present at the Mass, it was completely normal and acceptable to face the people instead of the tabernacle; it was all I knew.

Slowly, I started to ask questions about why the priest would do this. Like the silence, this action of the priest communicated a sense of self-denial. It was very clear as I watched all of the gestures of the priest, that he knew very well Who the Mass was about. Instead of talking to the congregation, the priest turned towards Christ with the congregation, symbolizing that we were called to offer ourselves with the priest in union with Christ's sacrifice. I could tell that, although he was not speaking to us aside from the occasional "Oremus," he was leading us by example, showing us whom we ought to be speaking to.

A few months after I had first attended the Traditional Latin Mass, Dad decided that we should start going not only to the Low Mass on Fridays, but also to the High Mass on Sundays and fully switch from our Novus Ordo parish to full-time Latin Mass parishioners. The first time I walked into a TLM on a Sunday, I was shocked because I saw so many families everywhere. This was a drastically huge difference from my previous parish which had been predominantly elderly people minus the few families who showed up for Christmas and Easter Mass. I remember being so happy that there were so many young kids my age who also went to Sunday Mass.

Since Dad had forewarned me before Mass, I knew that this "High Mass" was going to be different from the Low Mass I had gotten used to. When Mass had begun, in the place of the silence of Low Mass, the Church was filled with the angelic sound of Gregorian Chant and polyphonic pieces by Palestrina and Byrd all sung by an amazing choir. This could not even compare to any music I had ever heard at a Mass for a First-Class Feast let alone a normal Sunday Mass. Although the sacred music was in Latin and I could not understand every word that was being sung, the beauty of the chant made me finally understand St. Augustine's quote: "Singing is praying twice." I distinctly remember right after receiving communion hearing Biebl's *Ave Maria* for the first time. The beauty of the piece allowed me to better lift my mind to God in prayer in a way that was very different from the silence of Low Mass, but still every bit as beautiful. The Traditional Latin Mass allowed me to fall in love with the sacred music of the Church in a way that hymns I had heard growing up with the Novus Ordo (such as *Somebody's Knocking on Your Door*, and *Amazing Grace*) simply could not do.

After becoming a full-time parishioner at a Traditional Latin Mass parish, I started to see just how important the Traditions of the Church truly are. My family slowly began to implement many practices which sadly today, many Catholics have strayed from such as daily Rosary, frequent Confession, and the reception of Holy Communion on the tongue. All of these basic fundamental Catholic practices helped me to better understand why Tradition is so important. I now understood what it meant to live a Catholic life; it means conforming your life to Christ as so many have before first and foremost through the Mass as a sacred liturgy.

Most importantly, the beautiful Latin liturgy helped me to fully understand the Mass as the representation of Calvary. I was always taught growing up that the Mass was a sacrifice of bread and wine which truly become Christ; while this is completely true, I had the misconception that every time the priest said the words of the consecration, there was a sort of new crucifixion, separate from every other Mass being said throughout the world. Why should I think otherwise, when every time I attended a Novus Ordo, the priest would add his own personal flair. When I started attending Latin Mass, I learned that every time the priest says the words of consecration over the bread and wine, the miracle which takes place transcends both space and time, for the sacrifice being made at the Mass is one with the sacrifice of Calvary. The traditional liturgy offered a beautiful sense of consistency. While of course there will always be slight differences in every Mass, there is always peace in knowing that even if I was attending the Latin Mass on the other side of the world, it would be no different than if I were at my home parish. Finally, I understood the significance of having a universal liturgy in a universal language. Now every time I go to Mass, I am so grateful for the opportunity to attend the Traditional Latin Mass, the same Mass that so many Catholics throughout history from all around the world have attended. I pray that one day, the whole Church will remember this beautiful tradition and once again join in the *una voce* of the Traditional Latin Mass.